RISK
MANAGEMENT

An Accountability Guide for
University and College Boards

Janice M. Abraham

Since 1921, the Association of Governing Boards of Universities and Colleges (AGB) has had one mission: to strengthen and protect this country's unique form of institutional governance through its research, services, and advocacy. Serving more than 1,250 member boards, nearly 2,000 institutions, and 38,000 individuals, AGB is the only national organization providing university and college presidents, board chairs, trustees, and board professionals of both public and private institutions and institutionally related foundations with resources that enhance their effectiveness.

In accordance with its mission, AGB has developed programs and services that strengthen the partnership between the president and governing board; provide guidance to regents and trustees; identify issues that affect tomorrow's decision making; and foster cooperation among all constituencies in higher education. For more information, visit *www.agb.org*.

United Educators Insurance (UE), a Reciprocal Risk Retention Group, is a licensed insurance company owned and governed by more than 1,200 member colleges, universities, independent schools, and public school districts throughout the United States. Members range from small private schools to multi-campus public universities. UE partners with its members to reduce risk through education-specific insurance coverage and risk management programs. UE's comprehensive suite of risk management resources includes blended learning programs designed to engage the entire campus community—faculty, staff, and students—in managing risk. For more information, visit *www.ue.org*.

RISK MANAGEMENT: AN ACCOUNTABILITY GUIDE FOR UNIVERSITY AND COLLEGE BOARDS

Copyright © 2013 by AGB Press, the Association of Governing Boards of Universities and Colleges, and United Educators Insurance, a Reciprocal Risk Retention Group

AGB | 1133 20th St. N.W., Suite 300 | Washington, DC 20036 | 202.296.8400 | *www.agb.org*
UE | Two Wisconsin Circle, Fourth Floor | Chevy Chase, MD 20815 | 301.215.8462 | *www.ue.org*

Library of Congress Control Number: 2013004523
ISBN 978-0-926508-73-6 (alk. paper)

For more information on AGB Press publications or to order additional copies of this book call 800.356-6317 or visit the AGB website at *www.agb.org/publications*.

CONTENTS

FOREWORD

The Association of Governing Boards of Universities and Colleges (AGB) and United Educators (UE) recently conducted surveys on how university and college boards apply principles of risk assessment in setting institutional policy and carrying out their fiduciary oversight. Findings were mixed and a bit surprising. Only one third of the boards have formal processes in place for assessing risk. The results stand out because so many of the men and women who serve on governing bodies come from the corporate sector, where risk assessment is an accepted part of decision making. Clearly, more work is needed to make risk assessment part of the standard protocol for higher education governance. *Risk Management: An Accountability Guide for University and College Boards* provides a way forward.

In this new and robust book, UE's president and CEO, Janice Abraham, presents a practical and proven process for boards to provide leadership and oversight in risk management and for administrations to conduct enterprise risk management (ERM). In order to manage risk effectively, risk must first be defined broadly—those risks that have negative consequences and those that offer positive opportunities. Determining a level of risk tolerance requires an engaged board that works in collaboration with institutional leaders to assess critical institutional areas, such as academic quality, emergency preparedness, intercollegiate athletics, and governance itself.

Over time, in higher education, the stakes have risen and risk-related issues have become more complex. Operational risks include not just alcohol abuse, student health, and campus security, but also faculty tenure, research integrity, and fi-

"This is a story about the responsibility boards have to explore, with institutional leaders, those risks and opportunities that can be anticipated as well as those that are unknown unknowns. It is about asking good questions and imagining the unimaginable."

nancial aid and enrollment management. Financial risks run the gamut from debt, investments, and regulatory compliance to fundraising activities and financial modeling. And, an expanding set of cross-functional strategic risks are related to crisis response, global programs, community and government relations, and computer systems and security.

A word about board governance risks: Risk assessment also requires the board to regularly monitor its own performance and evaluate its effectiveness. Standard risk metrics and heat maps should include a candid look at board practices and policies, including conflicts of interest, board composition, and presidential assessment, among others. Governance done well can help support institutional change and transformation. Failed or ineffective governance can have a sustained negative impact on the institution and across higher education. Boards send a symbolic yet very real message of how seriously they take their responsibilities when they include the standards of fiduciary principles on the list of risks that require vigilance.

Janice appropriately reminds us that the challenge is how best to balance risk avoidance with risk tolerance. She also reminds us that risk is an institution-wide responsibility, not just the province of the administration or, at the board level, the audit committee. Perhaps the most important responsibility for a board is to establish policies and practices that bring risk assessment into board and committee meetings so that institutional decisions will be informed by an understanding of the attendant risk factors.

I can think of no one better to address risk management than Janice. This book benefits not just from her work with UE's client institutions, but from her profound passion for higher education, deep commitment to good governance, and multifaceted perspectives as a CEO and board member. AGB is grateful to Janice, her colleagues at UE, and the other experts she interviewed for developing this important contribution to the field of board governance.

In the end, this is a story about the responsibility boards have to explore, with institutional leaders, those risks and opportunities that can be anticipated as well as those that are unknown unknowns. It is about asking good questions and imagining the unimaginable. How much risk—upside or downside—can we tolerate? These are very appropriate conversations for boards. Ultimately, this process of strategic inquiry and rigorous exploration of risk is central to good governance. And, good governance, by its very nature, requires genuine collaboration between the board and administrative and academic leadership.

As part of its ongoing pursuit of accountability in higher education, AGB remains committed to more formal risk identification and oversight by boards. *Risk Management* presents practical tools for a more intentional, inclusive approach to ERM that is grounded in common sense and good governance. We encourage you to apply the concepts and adapt the tools contained in this book to your governance model.

Richard D. Legon
President
Association of Governing Boards of Universities and Colleges
April 2013

PREFACE

Just when I think I have seen it all, something happens that surprises me.

Over my more than 30-year career serving education, I have become well aware of the bad things that can happen at a college or university. Incidents related to alcohol, hazing, and athletic scandals, while thankfully not common, also are not so obscure as to be outside of the realm of possibility.

But when a tenure denial leads to an incident of workplace violence, or sexual allegations are made, or a shooting incident occurs on campus, I'm disheartened. Equally alarming is a culture that exists on too many campuses that protects individuals and traditions, ignores ethics and values, and leaves the most vulnerable at great risk of harm. Trustees, administrators, faculty, staff, students, and alumni all have roles to play in questioning even sacred cows. No individual or tradition should be exempt from precautionary policies—not athletic stars, future (or current) Nobel laureates, a beloved Mr. Chips, tailgating, nor initiation rites.

Left unheeded, societal trends of shifting demographics, declining state support, and competition from new education providers are also emerging risks for colleges and universities. Some trends are not necessarily risks or crises, until they are. Advising higher education administrators and board members on how to best prevent bad things from happening consumes much of my time and is the purpose of this book.

In my career and volunteer work, I move between the two distinct worlds of running a business that serves higher education and serving as a college trustee. As a former administrator at a large research university and a liberal arts college, I try to be deliberate and intentional in remembering which hat I am wearing in these different roles. Transitioning between the two worlds of business and volunteer service can be difficult for any board member; the labyrinth-like decision making process at colleges and universities can be challenging and sometimes frustrating. "High velocity" is not a term frequently ascribed to higher education administration or governance, but it seems more relevant today than at any other time in my long service to education. Balancing mission and change is the challenge for all who serve in education. The core values of higher education—the focus on mission, long-term horizon, and shared decision making—serve institutions well. Retaining these values, while being more intentional and focused on risks and change, is our challenge.

As a trustee, I, like many of you, prefer to focus energy on the upside of risk. Guiding the college or university in taking strategic risks is a large part of the board's role. Adding new programs, building new facilities, or rebranding the institution can help ensure appropriate long-term enrollment levels, endowment funding, and community support. I encourage you to continue your oversight of strategic risk-taking, inspiring administrators to think broadly as they shape the future of their institutions.

I also encourage you to pay greater attention to other risks on campus—the risk of bad things happening—that can tarnish the institution's reputation and negatively impact the ability to achieve its mission. Too often, board members are unaware of the risks inherent in higher education. This is not due to an intentional lack of interest or attention to important risks, but rather to a lack of understanding. For too many colleges and universities, risks are unappreciated, cross-functional risks have no clear oversight responsibility, and mitigation plans are either not put into practice or are ineffective.

This book lays out principles and a process for the board to support a culture within the institution that embraces and prepares for risk. It is also designed to help senior administrators develop and support the board in providing appropriate board oversight and responses related to a myriad of risks. After reading this book, board members should be able to:

1. **Support college and university administrators in implementing a streamlined process to identify, assess, manage, and report risks.**

Part I introduces the importance of institutional risk management, an Enterprise Risk Management (ERM) process model that administrators can use to assess and manage institution-wide risks and the external and internal forces that shape the risk environment for higher education. A good ERM program executed by senior administration should result in reports raised to and addressed at a board level on the most critical risks to achieving an institution's strategic plan and/or mission.

2. **Understand the complexity and breadth of risks colleges and universities face and engage in meaningful discussions with campus leaders—asking the difficult questions that will help the administration better manage risks.** Part II introduces specific risks that are likely to appear on most "risk registers" used by college and university administrators to identify, assess, and plan for risks during an ERM process. The background information and questions provided equip trustees with both context and the right questions to ask to help ensure that administrators are closing gaps and focusing on the right issues.

> **"**As a trustee, I, like many of you, prefer to focus energy on the upside of risk. Guiding the college or university in taking strategic risks is a large part of the board's role.**"**

One additional comment on vocabulary: I am well aware of the different preferences within higher education, but for the sake of simplicity, I have used the following titles and designations throughout this book:

- *Institution* refers to a college, university, system, or institutionally related foundation. (Because foundations do not have direct responsibility for academics, certain sections of this book may not be relevant for their boards and administrative teams.)
- *Board member* refers to the individuals who serve on the board. In practice, they may be called trustees, regents, governors, or directors.
- *President* refers to the chief executive at the helm of the institution. This person may be the president of an independent institution, chancellor of a public institution or system, or executive director of a foundation.

Not every risk discussed here will be relevant to every college, university, system, or foundation, and your institution's leadership may identify additional risks not discussed here. But if this book serves as an introduction to the world of higher education risks, fosters an appreciation for the tough jobs higher education administrators face, and challenges boards to take risk management seriously, I will have accomplished what I set out to do.

Part I
FUNDAMENTALS OF RISK MANAGEMENT

" The word 'risk' derives from the
early Italian *risicare* which means
'to dare.' In this sense, risk is a
choice rather than a fate."

— Peter L. Bernstein, author of *Against the Gods:
The Remarkable Story of Risk*

1

GOOD RISK MANAGEMENT IS GOOD GOVERNANCE

" In the future we will look at risks affecting the whole of an organization and its place in the community. We will address both upside and downside consequences, and our view will be enterprise-wide, integrated and holistic. The result will be a more intelligent balance between potential benefits and harms. We will increase the confidence of stakeholders in our organizations and make them more resilient in a day and age of increased uncertainty. This is the real goal of risk management. "
—Felix Kloman, founder and editor of *Risk Management Reports*

The future is here. Risk management is at its core a governance and management discipline, not an end but a means to the end, with the end being the accomplishment of the institution's mission. What is risk management from the board's perspective? Just as good financial management is more than a clean audit opinion, good risk management is more than not getting sued and having adequate insurance policies in place. Effective risk management prepares an institution to weather literal and figurative storms and sets the course for accomplishing the institution's strategic plan.

Whether you have just been appointed to a board position, or have long served as a board member for a college or university, you no doubt recognize the increasing burden being placed on boards for better institutional oversight.

When things go wrong, the board should have known. Even if the wrong-doing falls out of the scope of traditional board responsibility, finger pointing by the media, parents, students, and others now means that every board must have a thorough understanding of the risks at its academic institution and up-to-date knowledge of how well the administration is working to mitigate those risks.

Colleges and universities have a strong track record of successfully weathering catastrophic events, which speaks to their resilience and historic place in society. But today's environment is different. The rapid pace of change and innovation, the 24/7 news cycle and insatiable appetite for information, the litigation climate, and increasing scrutiny by regulators all place more pressure on boards to get it right. Boards must set the tone for the importance of risk management. While it is unlikely that a single long-term trend or catastrophic event will close an institution, the margin of error is significantly narrower when financial reserves are low and students have more alternatives for pursuing their studies.

Benign neglect or poor preparation for major risks can weaken and undermine an institution, leaving a diminished reputation, an inability to respond, and unfulfilled plans embraced by the community. Boards are most effective if they operate with a clear set of priorities and concentrate on strategic oversight. Risk management should be on every board's to-do list for oversight.

The Role of Risk Management

With the myriad demands resting on the shoulders of boards and senior administrators, it is reasonable to ask: Why invoke risk management as yet another process in a process-laden structure? Will it really make a difference in how the institution plans or functions?

While no one can effectively calculate the total cost of risk, consider these costs of failing to prepare for events that history proves are inevitable:

- **What were the opportunity costs** as the board and senior leadership huddled in meetings to chart a recovery after a significant risk was realized?
- **How much money was spent**, not covered by insurance or outside sources, to try to speed the recovery?
- **What was the loss of promising faculty** who decided to accept a competing offer?

- **How many decisions to enroll elsewhere** were made by people who might have been future alumni?
- **Which donors held back on major gifts** until the institution could sort things out?
- **How did rating agencies respond?** Was a bond rating lowered, or not raised, in turn raising questions about the financial strength of the institution?
- **How much additional effort must now be expended to instill future confidence** in the institution?[1]

An effective institutional or enterprise risk management (ERM) program, with the full support and engagement of the governing board, will increase a college, university, or system's likelihood of achieving its plans, increase transparency, and allow better allocation of scarce resources. Good risk management is good governance.

Evolution of Risk Management

The field of risk management is evolving. The transformation began in the late 20th century, when the focus was risk transfer and loss control, and an institution's exposure to losses drove the thinking about risk management. Where could the institution suffer a loss, usually defined by a lawsuit, fire, flood, or accident? How could the institution reduce its exposure? Addressing these questions meant buying insurance and signing contracts with service providers to transfer risks. Campus loss control focused on safety, physical injury from slips and falls, and property damage from natural disasters.

ERM in Higher Education

Enterprise risk management took hold in the corporate world in the early years of the 21st century. Models developed by the Committee of Sponsoring Organizations of the Treadway Commission (COSO) and the International Standards Organization (ISO) established the framework that is the foundation for most ERM

---

[1] For additional resources from AGB, see Schwartz, Merrill. "The Big Risk in Not Assessing Risk." *Trusteeship*, January/February 2012.

practices today. The goal of ERM was, and is, to move away from viewing risk in silos and instead look across the enterprise for risks. ERM advanced to colleges and universities as governing board members brought their business experiences to higher education boardrooms. As they worked with ERM in their businesses and on corporate boards, they began to recognize the applicability and relevance of using a holistic approach to risk management in academic institutions.[2] The COSO framework assigns risks to one of four categories: strategic, operations, reporting, or compliance. Many in higher education modified these categories to strategic, operations, finance, and compliance. If any of these risks occur on a major scale, reputational risk is sure to follow.

In today's environment, ERM is a combination of strategic planning, traditional risk management, and internal controls. A consensus definition, and one used for this book, is the following:

> **Enterprise Risk Management (ERM)** is a business process, led by senior leadership, that extends the concepts of risk management and includes:
> - Identifying risks across the entire enterprise;
> - Assessing the impact of risks to the operations and mission;
> - Developing and practicing response or mitigation plans; and
> - Monitoring the identified risks, holding the risk owner accountable, and consistently scanning for emerging risks.

Moving Forward

The evolution of risk management continues today as both a grassroots and grass tops initiative. Best practice now is to have broad-based ownership of risk management from top to bottom and throughout the institution. The board and president jointly articulate a commitment to risk management, and the senior administration implements an enterprise-wide process of identifying and analyzing risks and communicating and increasing awareness about risks across the institution's operation. The focus now is on establishing roles and responsibilities so that everyone

---

[2] For additional resources from AGB, see Alexander, Lamar. "What Do American Auto Manufacturers and Higher Ed Have in Common?" *Trusteeship*, January/February 2012.

on campus considers risk in their day-to-day activities.

The board has a role in this evolving risk management model: to engage senior leadership and integrate risk management into the work of board committees and full board deliberations, and to require risk management discussion as part of major program and project reviews and strategic planning. Board discussions need to consider both the upside of risk (opportunities to enhance the institution's mission and operations) and the downside of risk (what could happen to prevent the institution from accomplishing its plans and achieving its mission). How intentionally a board and administration think about risk, and how well they respond when the unexpected occurs, is the ultimate test of a sound risk management program.

Insight: All Risk is *Not* Local

How has risk management evolved on campuses? "Over recent decades, risk management has moved beyond the campus to the larger community of Ithaca, then over state borders to where it is now, encompassing global programs run by Cornell—all with regular oversight by the board."

—Allen Bova, long-time director of risk management (retired), Cornell University

2

ENTERPRISE RISK MANAGEMENT: A GUIDE FOR ADMINISTRATORS

Institution-wide or enterprise risk management (ERM) should be part of every institution's operations and planning.[3] An institution that has not established an ERM discipline and structure is comparable to an institution without a plan. Without the discipline of identifying risks, assigning ownership, consulting with subject matter experts, and monitoring progress to reduce the risks, institutions will fall behind when the inevitable crisis occurs. ERM also supports an institution taking on new programs and initiatives with the confidence that risks have been vetted and communicated. ERM is a discipline for campus administrators, led by the president, for risk identification, assessment, mitigation, and reporting responsibilities and, ultimately, to inform board members of the most significant institutional risks *(see Exhibit 1)*.

Step 1: Risk Identification—Compiling a Risk Register

Risks can be identified in many ways, but starting from a blank slate is the least efficient. After more than a decade of ERM programs on campuses, many comprehensive lists exist that can be used as a starting point. Many institutions spend too much time involving large numbers of faculty and staff in identifying a long list of

---

[3] For additional resources from AGB, see Abraham, Janice M. "Vitiating Vulnerability." *Trusteeship*, September/October 2007.

Exhibit 1: **Key Steps in Enterprise Risk Management (ERM)**

1	2	3	4
Risk Identification	**Risk Assessment**	**Risk Mitigation Plan**	**Report to Board**

• Senior Risk Committee (Administration)
• Risk Registers
	• Risk Score=Impact x Likelihood
	• Immediacy of Risk
		• Assign Owner
		• Consult Risk Subject Matter Expert
		• Reduce Risk Score
			• Committee
			  – Specific, Standing
			  – Audit
			  – Executive
			• Full Board

---

100 to 200 risks but little time and energy to do the real work of thoughtfully assessing them and then developing treatment or mitigation plans.

The risk identification process led by senior administrators should identify no more than 20 key risks across the institution. Of the top 20 risks identified by the senior administration, approximately 10 should be reported to the board and its committees. Experience shows that focus is diluted and follow-through is weak if an institution's risk register is more than that. *(See Exhibit 2 and Appendix A.)*

Institutions with the greatest success in incorporating risk management into ongoing operations and involving the board at the appropriate point report that they start small. They begin with a group of knowledgeable individuals at a senior level within the administration—a senior risk management committee—and use existing lists of risks to identify, assess, mitigate, and monitor the top risks. *(See Exhibit 2 and Appendix B.)*

A senior risk committee, working across the campus at the administrative level, is an essential starting point for effective ERM. *(See Appendix B for a sample committee charter.)* While the process of risk identification can be repeated and extended to the broader community in future years, the board should gain comfort that the biggest risks, the risks with the

Insight: Invert the 80/20 rule

Institutions tend to spend 80 percent of their risk management time identifying risks and 20 percent doing something about those risks, such as assessing the impact of risks, assigning owners to the risks, developing plans to reduce risk, and tracking risk. But best practice calls for reversing the 80-20 allocation of effort. Using the lists in this book and gleaned from other institutions, institutions can jump-start the risk identification process and limit it to 20 percent of the effort. Spending the remaining 80 percent on assessing the likelihood, impact, and risk mitigation strategies (rather than reinventing the work done by others) is a far more efficient use of everyone's time.

greatest likelihood of severely impact-ing the mission and ongoing opera-tions of the institution, are addressed first and brought forward for the board's review.

Risk identification is not a "one and done" exercise but a process that should be incorporated into the ongo-ing governance and management of an institution. Administrators should also use ERM for new programs and initiatives, using its risk identification, assessment, and mitigation process to assess business plans for a new aca-demic program, a capital campaign, or a joint venture.

Ideally, the risk identification process is repeated or reviewed every two years or as events dictate. In sub-sequent years, after the top risks are identified and the board and senior ad-

Who serves on the senior risk management committee?

A senior group of administrators, with experience and accountability across the functions of the institution, is best positioned to serve as a risk management team and risk owners.

Senior risk management committees often consist of the chief academic officer, general counsel, and officers from such areas as student affairs, technology, development, athletics, finance, and administration. Adding a campus risk manager, internal auditor, and compliance officer to this group of senior administrators can augment its expertise.[4] Some campuses also include vice presidents of facilities, research, campus police, investments, and/or the medical director as part of the senior risk management committee.

This team will provide the breadth and depth needed to identify, assess, and assign ownership of the top risks facing the institution. Ownership by a senior administrator of each risk is important as it creates accountability and responsibility for developing mitigation plans, testing the plans, and monitoring adherence to the plans.

[4] For additional resources from AGB, see White, Lawrence. "Five Unsung Campus Heroes Every Trustee Should Know (or Know About)." *Trusteeship*, May/June 2012.

ministration gain confidence in the process, going deeper into the institution to identify additional risks is recommended. Members of the campus risk committee can conduct focus groups and individual interviews with campus managers and faculty leaders. Asking "What keeps you up at night?" and similar questions can be a revealing process for grassroots risk identification. This approach offers the opportunity to uncover potential risks that the central administration may not have recognized as significant. If a broader net of grassroots risk identification process is initiated, the campus must be prepared to embark on the next steps of assessing the risks and developing risk-mitigation plans for each risk identified. *Identifying risks without the appropriate follow-through could create potential liability expo-sure and a credibility gap in the community.*

Exhibit 2: **Sample Risk Registers**

To start the process of risk identification, use the risk registers currently in use by institutions to build your own risk register.

Public Research University
Risk Register

1) Economic conditions and base funding
2) Enrollment growth
3) Human resources process and leadership
4) IT infrastructure
5) Physical infrastructure
6) Progressive faculty renewal
7) Relationships with key supporters
8) Reputation
9) Research growth, complexity
10) Safety and security

Independent Research University
Risk Register *(Example 1)*

1) Effectiveness and efficiency of financial operations
2) Facilities renewal and optimization
3) Adequacy of human capital
4) Conflicts of interest
5) Disruption of operations
6) Fundraising sufficiency
7) Health and safety
8) Regulatory compliance
9) Sponsored research—volume uncertainty
10) Student success

Independent Research University
"Red and Yellow" Ranked
Risk Register *(Example 2)*

1) Financial stewardship
   a. Medical billing compliance
   b. Financial fraud
   c. Subsidiaries and affiliates
2) Safety and security
   a. IT Security and systems recovery
   b. Patient safety and medical malpractice
   c. Environmental health and safety
   d. International programs
3) Research programs
   a. Protection of research subjects
   b. Integrity of research results
   c. Allocation of employee effort
   d. Conflicts of interest
   e. Care of animals
4) Employment Issues
   a. Professional misconduct
   b. Conflicts of interest
   c. Discrimination
   d. Sexual harassment

Independent Comprehensive University
Risk Register

1) Academic quality (including faculty retirement planning)
2) Budgeting and forecasting
3) Community safety
4) Compliance risk
5) Decentralization
6) Deferred maintenance
7) Enrollment management/retention
8) Financial aid
9) Financial stability
10) Political and regulatory change
11) Branding strategy

Source: The above samples are actual risk registers gathered from a variety of institutions of different sizes and types. While many risks are common among institutions, many differences also exist; these lists are designed to be copied, modified, and used to start Step 1 of the ERM process.

Independent Liberal Arts College
Risk Register

1) Enrollment: Students' perceived return on investment for education
2) Succession planning for president and senior staff
3) Facilities: Age and condition not keeping pace with student demand for residential living and increased interest in science
4) Health and safety of students, focused on alcohol consumption
5) Information technology infrastructure, security and renewal
6) Endowment growth

Public University System
Risk Register *(Example 1)*

1) Adequacy of financial resources
2) Information technology infrastructure, systems and support
3) Age and condition of facilities and physical plant infrastructure
4) Recruitment and retention of top personnel
5) Individual and institutional conflict of interest, employee misconduct, regulatory non-compliance

Public University System
Risk Register *(Example 2)*

1) Governance: System wide and institutional goals, roles and methods
2) Student enrollment
3) Government support
4) Liquidity, debt, and reserves
5) Health care costs
6) Employee morale
7) Management turnover
8) Return on investment in new capital projects and programs
9) Legal/regulatory compliance
10) Information security
11) Disaster recovery and business continuity
12) Potential for fraud and conflicts of interest

Community College
Risk Register

1) Reputational risk: Inconsistent messaging and application of procedures
2) Strategic risk: Aging workforce, lack of succession planning, large number of looming retirements
3) Financial risk: Current funding and capital needs
4) Operational risk: Lack of disaster preparedness, business continuity plans
5) Operational risk: Minors on campus
6) Strategic risk: Misalignment between operations and strategic plans
7) Operational risk: Lack of data custodian/control of data
8) Operational risk: Outside violence coming to campus
9) Financial risk: Further state budget cuts
10) Operational risk: Wasteful and duplicative spending

Institutionally Related Foundation
Risk Register

1) Changing state legislation and regulation
2) Fiduciary: Investment of endowment, financial reporting and disclosure requirements
3) Economic climate reduces donations
4) Failure to follow established procedures and policies separating foundation from university
5) Succession planning for leadership
6) IT and data security
7) Crisis response plans
8) Coordination and alignment with other groups supporting university (alumni association, boosters, etc.)

Insight: Don't overlook small programs with over-sized risks

Risk identification that only looks at big-budget or well-known programs runs the risk of missing nascent entrepreneurial efforts or small programs that could create over-sized risks. One campus administrator recalled that the key strategic risks for the institution had been developed and reported to the board and committees. It seemed that all was well from an ERM standpoint. In a subsequent meeting with the education department, a small program that cost the campus very little money was mentioned. For years, the program had been operating off the radar screen of the central administration. The program served underprivileged youth from the community, partnering university students with the children. Because the program was so small and unnoticed, appropriate training, background checks, and other risk mitigation practices were not in place, leaving unsupervised students and staff working closely with vulnerable children.

Step 2: Risk Assessment—Scoring the Risks

After identifying the risks, the next step for senior administrators is to assess 1) the likelihood that the risk or event will occur and 2) the impact it could have on the institution's ongoing operation. This sorting and classification process establishes a road map for administrators to identify the strategic risks that should be shared with the board.

Exhibit 3: **Simple Heat Map**

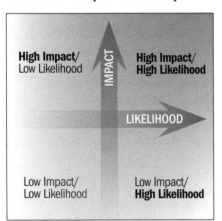

Risk assessment can be simple or complex, depending on available resources and culture of the institution. *It is not an exact science, but rather a process to develop priorities for the institution.* Colleges and universities use an array of different tools for assessing risk, from simple heat maps and worksheets to complex modeling spreadsheets and scenarios. For example, the senior risk committee of an institution with limited resources, using a simple heat map *(see Exhibit 3)*, can start by writing specific risks on sticky notes and placing the notes in the quadrant of a heat map to reflect the impact and probability of the risk. Placement of sticky notes depends on administrator's answers to the questions: "How likely is it that this will occur at our campus?" and "How bad will it be if it does?" The goal of this exercise is to identify the risks that belong in the "high impact/high likelihood" quadrant and begin risk mitigation plans on these risks first.

Exhibit 4: **Tool for Determining Total Risk Score (TRS)**

RISK		1-2. Insignificant/ Mild	3. Moderate	4-5. Significant/ Catastrophic	SCORE
(Describe risk here.)	**IMPACT**	Minimal impact on annual operations, reputation or financial condition.	Could delay plans in place, affect short-term programs, and require moderate management effort; 1-6 months' recovery.	Long-term and significant effect on ability to recruit students, faculty, financial support; material breach of confidence and reputation.	(Assign number 1–5)
		1-2. Unlikely	**3. More Likely**	**4-5. High Probability**	X
	LIKELIHOOD	Unlikely to happen in the near future and no immediate action is needed.	More than likely to occur and management should begin to mitigate.	High probability event/risk will occur within a year; immediate action plans needed.	(Assign number 1–5)
					=
				TOTAL RISK SCORE	

(Impact x Likelihood = TRS)

For institutions with more resources, a more complex risk assessment method involves the use of a scoring tool *(see Exhibit 4)*.[5]

By assigning risks an *Impact* and *Likelihood* score and then multiplying them, administrators can compute a *Total Risk Score* (TRS) for each risk considered. The Total Risk Score, however, should not be a substitute for good judgment of the senior administration. While the TRS is a quantitative ranking, senior risk committee members should use their professional judgment to evaluate the ranking, reordering as appropriate and grouping into High, Medium, or Low (or Red, Yellow, or Green). This kind of ranking process helps institutions spend scarce resources on their greatest vulnerabilities, and not waste time and energy on risks that pose only minor threats to the institution.

The top five to ten risks should be shared with the governing board and the

---

[5] For additional resources from AGB, see Pelletier, Stephen G. "New Strategies for Managing Risks: A Balancing Act for Boards." *Trusteeship*, January/February 2012.

appropriate board committee. The president and board chair should decide how the board will engage and conduct further inquiry into each risk. The second 10 to 20 risks should be assigned to department heads and deans with responsibility for developing mitigation plans and reporting regularly to the senior risk management committee.

Using a Heat Map Smartly: One Public System's Approach

"Risk Assessment was somewhat arbitrary and capricious within our system. So the system's general counsel and internal auditor met with all of the presidents of the campuses in the system and identified the top 12 risks," reports the chancellor of a public system. "Working with my staff, we ranked each risk based on probability of the risk occurring and impact if it did. We shared our ranking with the presidents and a wider group. And, after some discussion, we agreed that getting the risks in the correct quadrant (of the heat map) was important but we wanted to spend more time on the risk mitigation and risk planning, not arguing over the exact risk score."

Exhibit 5: **Sample Heat Map of a State System**

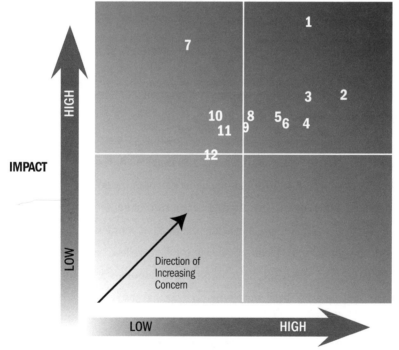

1. Student enrollment
2. Management turnover
3. Governance
4. Government support
5. Health care costs
6. Employee morale
7. Disaster recovery and business continuity
8. ROI in new initiatives and capital projects
9. Information security
10. Liquidity
11. Legal/regulatory compliance
12. Potential for fraud and conflicts of interest

PROBABILITY of future negative event over next 1–3 years

Risk Tolerance and Residual Risk

Part of the assessment process is understanding and articulating the institution's appetite for risk—How much risk is the institution willing to accept? This is sometimes called risk tolerance. A board can agree, for example, that an institution's finances can absorb a 10 percent decline in enrollment or a rise in interest rates of its variable rate bonds by 300 basis points. The board can ask for mitigation plans that address risks outside of that tolerance level.

It is unrealistic (and probably cost-prohibitive) to have a plan to reduce the impact or likelihood of *all* risks to zero. The best risk management mitigation plans should strive to reduce the likelihood and impact to a level that would not disrupt the institution's plans and seriously damage the institution's reputation. *Residual risk* is the risk the institution is willing to accept after the risk mitigation plans are in place. Residual risks usually reside in levels 1 and 2 *(see Exhibit 6)*. Legal counsel generally advises that it is not prudent to develop a risk tolerance score for health and safety risks, meaning that health and safety risks all require appropriate mitigation plans.

A goal of ERM is to have risk tolerance equal residual risk. The risk descriptions in Exhibit 6 can be used to rank scored risks into tolerance levels so that

---

Exhibit 6: **Levels of Risk Tolerance**

Level 4 (Risk Score 16 – 25): Will not accept this risk. Risk treatment must be established immediately such that the residual risk is at Level 3 or below. In general, these risks should be shared with the board as they will be strategic risks.

Level 3 (Risk Score 9 – 15): Will accept a risk at Level 3 as long as it is reduced in the mid-term through reasonable and practicable risk treatments.

Level 2 (Risk Score 5 – 8): Will accept a risk at Level 2 as long as it is reduced in the long-term using low resource options. The risk should be analyzed to determine whether it is being over-managed and where the control strategies could be relaxed in order to redeploy resources.

Level 1 (Risk Score 1 – 4): Requires no additional risk treatment. The risk should be analyzed to determine whether it is being over-managed and that control strategies can be relaxed in order to redeploy resources.

administrators can allocate resources to manage or mitigate risks based on the institution's risk tolerance. Risk scores and tolerance levels should be reported to the board committees.

Step 3: Risk Mitigation—Developing Risk Plans

Risk mitigation is best described as problem-solving. An event or trend has been identified that could either present great opportunities or seriously hinder the operations and plans of the institution. The challenge for the campus is: What course correction should be invoked to capitalize on or reduce the risk?

Textbook risk management definitions offer three options after risks are identified and assessed:

1. **Risk is transferred or shared**, either through purchasing an insurance policy or signing a contract with a third party. *Example:* The university purchases insurance to replace buildings in the event of fire. *(See Appendix C.)*

2. **Risk is eliminated** because the program or risk is discontinued. *Example:* The president declines a grant to support a new research center because the risk of not securing long-term support after the five-year grant expires is too great.

3. **Risk is accepted, but changes are made** to mitigate and reduce the risk. *Example:* Facing a sharply rising and unsustainable increase in the discount rate, the college changes its financial aid package to reduce the discount rate and preserve the diversity of the student body.

Administrators rarely are able to, or want to, eliminate risks by just saying no. And the strategic risks identified at the senior level and shared with the board rarely are able to be transferred to an insurance company or shared with an outside vendor. Most of the strategic risks come from external forces, beyond the control of the institution, but they still must be addressed and managed. Mitigation plans should be developed to move risks from Level 4 to Level 3 or lower. Best practices for risk mitigation include establishing ownership and accountability for each risk, either at the senior administrator or department and dean level.

"Risk management is a process not a product."

— Michael Liebowitz, director of risk management, New York University

Step 4: Monitoring and Risk Reports— Engaging the Board

Tracking and communicating the risks for board review is an often neglected but vital step in a sound ERM program. Monitoring and communicating risks answers the question of how well the institution is prepared to respond to issues and events that

---

Exhibit 7: **Sample Risk Management Report for the Board**

Date:	January 1, 20XX
Name of Risk:	Enrollment
Accountability:	Vice President, Admissions and Financial Aid
Board Committee:	Student Affairs
Description of Risk:	Applicant pool, admit rate, and yields all producing negative trends. High school graduates in tri-state region declining. Graduation rates below peer institutions.
Likelihood:	4 (Rate 1 – 5)
Impact:	5 (Rate 1 – 5)
Risk Score	20 (Likelihood x Impact) Level 4
Risk Tolerance:	Level 3
Treatment/Mitigation:	Increase budget for high school junior name search, expand high school guidance counselor visits, open admission office in city in new area, research and present reports on success of recent college graduates in securing gainful employment, develop Return on Investment calculation to use in marketing to families of prospective students, increase funding for career center to help place students in internships and jobs upon graduation.
Likelihood After Treatment:	2
Impact After Treatment:	3
Risk Score After Treatment:	6 (Likelihood x Impact) Level 2

could derail its mission. A board risk report should be a short, concise document summarizing the nature of the risk, the campus owner, the risk score and tolerance level, mitigation plan, and risk score/tolerance level after the mitigation plan is in place *(see Exhibit 7)*. Board committee charters should clearly state the obligation to review and discuss—at least annually—risk mitigation plans presented by the administration. By providing annual reports on the risk mitigation strategies to the board and/or board committees, the committee is better positioned to hold the administration accountable and identify gaps in identification or plans.

ERM in Action

How ERM is put into practice varies, and it is often informed by the scale and scope of the enterprise. Comparing the process used by an individual university (University of Alberta) with that used by a statewide system (The University of Missouri System) helps illustrate this:

- **The University of Missouri System** assesses risks and assigns risk scores prior to risk mitigation plans and performs the same analysis after risk mitigation plans. The system also articulates its risk tolerance and continues to develop mitigation plans to move the risk score to be at or below the risk tolerance. The system office leads the process and involves campus presidents and senior staff in identifying, assessing, and mitigating the risks.

- **The University of Alberta** uses a continual loop focused on the university's top 10 institutional risks. The university uses internal and external subject matter experts inside and outside the university to identify risks. An internal ERM committee assesses the top risks and reports that assessment to the president's top administrative committee before reporting to the board audit committee. The audit committee then reviews the reports and incorporates risks into the university's annual audit plan as needed. Other board committees also regularly review and monitor risk in their respective areas (such as finance, safety, and human resources) and report to the full board. Then, the process begins again the following year *(see Exhibit 8)*.

Exhibit 8: **Sample Risk Management Process**

Top 10 Institutional Risks Update and Approval Cycle

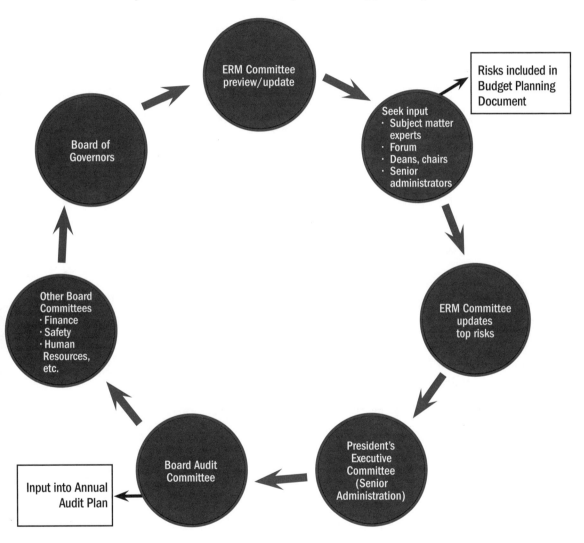

Adapted from the University of Alberta. Reprinted with permission.

3

EXTERNAL AND INTERNAL STAKEHOLDERS IN RISK MANAGEMENT

College and university leaders are not alone in efforts to monitor risks and weigh their impacts on the future of the institution. Students and prospective students, families and alumni, legislators, regulators, accrediting commissions, bond rating agencies, bond holders, audit firms, bankers, and the media—as well as every individual and entity with some stake or investment in an institution—are all watching to see whether the institution can survive and thrive as known and unknown risks occur at a dizzying speed. Each of these constituencies brings its own perspective and motivation to assess the institution's preparedness and resiliency.

External Stakeholders: Auditors, Accrediting Commissions, Rating Agencies, and Banks

In particular, audit firms, accrediting commissions, and lenders (including bond holders, rating agencies, and banks) have direct and prescriptive responsibilities in assessing the institution's long-term viability and preparedness. The board and administration can learn from and tap these external groups to support and enhance the risk management process.

Audit Firms and Outside Consultants

The cornerstone of a board's risk management and fiduciary responsibilities is an external review of financial statements and internal processes that is designed to ensure accuracy and completeness. A thorough review of management letters and accompanying reports and confidential discussion between the independent auditors and the audit committee supports the understanding and integrity of the representation of the institution's financial condition.

More recently, following the corporate trend of enterprise risk management (ERM), audit firms may be engaged as both internal auditors and ERM consultants. However, conflict of interest standards dictate that different firms should be engaged to perform the financial audit and ERM consultation. Firms and independent consultants with expertise in higher education are using this experience to develop processes in risk identification, risk assessment, and reporting to boards. Using color-coded heat maps, metrics, and key performance indicators to help boards understand and track important risks, these consultants bring expertise and a broad range of perspectives to help senior administrators initiate and maintain an ERM process.

At the same time, many institutions—large and small, research and liberal arts, community colleges and foundations—developing and implementing ERM use only internal resources. Administrators in these institutions advocate a home-grown approach to promote ownership of the process by senior administrators and to take advantage of their deep levels of expertise. Whether the institution decides to retain outside consulting expertise or embark on an ERM program internally, it can rest assured that both are viable options.

Accrediting Commissions

As a risk management tool, the accreditation process illuminates the strengths and weaknesses in the planning processes and the ability of the institution to deliver on its promise of a quality education. The goal of accreditation is to 1) ensure that the education provided by colleges and universities meets acceptable levels of quality and 2) help improve the quality through external review. The accreditation process focuses on evaluating an institution's ability to plan for academic success and student attainment and to measure the outcomes of the plan. In response to pressure, accreditors are increasing focus on risk management or how well the institution is able to respond to and recover from unplanned events.

The accreditation process addresses risk management more in concept than in specific criteria. But how an institution thinks about, prepares for, and responds to risks is increasingly important. According to Barbara Brittingham of the New England Association of Schools and Colleges (NEASC) Commission on Institutions of Higher Education, accrediting agencies are "using the concept of risk

> **" Accrediting agencies are using the concept of risk management more than we explicitly talk about. "**
>
> — Barbara Brittingham, New England Association of Schools and Colleges, Commission on Institutions of Higher Education

management more than we explicitly talk about." Specific references to evaluating risk management tend to focus on insured or financial risks and are more likely to be articulated in the standards governing the finances of an institution. Consider these accreditation standards:

- "Policies on risk management that address loss by fire, burglary, and defalcation; liability of the governing board and administration; and liability for personal injury and property damage" —*Western Association of Schools and Colleges*
- "In exercising its fiduciary responsibility, the governing board assures that senior officers identify, assess, and manage risk and ensure regulatory compliance." —*NEASC, Standard 3.7*

Accrediting commissions also are increasing the focus and review of an institution's plans for new programs and initiatives and the risks associated with new ventures. The accreditation self-studies and peer reviews look to see if the mission and goals of continuing and new programs are clearly defined and if contingency plans include a specific crisis response plan for unforeseen events.

Rating Agencies, Banks, and Bondholders

The principles of risk management are integral to reviews undertaken by rating agencies and banks as they evaluate the institution's ability to repay borrowed funds and interest. Banks, rating agencies, and, ultimately, bondholders evaluate the institution's ability to prepare for and respond to future external changes and shocks to the economy. They also evaluate the institution's ability to respond to longer-term risks, including succession planning, shifting demographics within an institution's traditional markets, and an institution's ability to develop and implement contingency plans.

The board and administration should also use the rating agency's or bank's report to identify emerging risks that may not be included on the institution's risk register. Currently, checklists of risk management practices used by rating agencies to evaluate a higher education institution do not exist. However, ongoing discussions within the financing community may, in the future, have the higher education sector follow the lead of corporate borrowers that integrate ERM into the review of the company prior to awarding a rating.

Rating agencies and investment banks are paying greater attention to bondholder concerns for increased transparency relating to financial information, planning documents, and metrics. The Municipal Securities Rulemaking Board's website (emma.msrb.org) broadens the exposure of financial disclosures required by institutions issuing publically traded debt. Public and independent universities, such as Harvard, Stanford, Texas Tech, University of San Diego, and Vanderbilt, are establishing websites to share relevant financial and planning documents with holders of their tax-exempt bonds. This trend will continue and intensify as transparency and risk management gains traction in all financial transactions.

Internal Stakeholders: The Board, Committees, and Task Forces

A clear understanding of the roles and responsibilities of all groups involved in developing a good risk management process will eliminate duplication of work and gaps in oversight and emphasize accountability.

The Role of Senior Leadership

As previously discussed, the *president/chancellor* and *senior administration* are responsible for performing the ERM process by identifying, managing, and monitoring risks. ERM is owned by the administration and provides an organized process to identify risks to be shared with the governing board and committees. Once senior administrators have completed the initial ERM risk identification process, they should inform the board of the risks that have the greatest potential impact on the institution and the greatest likelihood of occurring. It is important to remember that ERM is never complete but an ongoing activity that evolves and integrates into the institution as the years pass.

The Role of the Board

Governing boards have the responsibility of setting the correct tone and demonstrating strong commitment to a robust risk management process but should refrain from actually developing the process or risk mitigation strategies. The *full board's* actions and words should encourage candor and transparency on risks. Boards should discourage the administration from only bringing positive issues forward, ignoring the gnarly, complex risks.

Board Committees

Board committees should take responsibility for oversight of the most important strategic risks that fall within each committee's defined purview *(see Exhibit 9)*.[6] For high priority risks that do not fall neatly within a single committee's assigned role, and/or risks that transcend the charge of multiple committees, there are three routes to choose from:

- The **full board** addresses these risks.
- A **task force** is appointed to monitor specific risks (such as board task forces on technology or diversity) and report its work to the full board.
- The **executive committee** performs the oversight role of risks that are not assigned to a standing committee and reports its work to the full board.

For example, while admissions is often assigned to the student affairs committee, the rise in the discount rate, desire to increase the diversity of the student body,

Insight: Boards should keep "noses in, fingers out" in ERM

Frank Rhodes, president emeritus of Cornell University, often referred to the concept of "noses in and fingers out." That is also good advice for boards in how they approach risk management. The concept refers to the ability to sniff out risks and stay aware of trends while relying on the administration to provide appropriate and timely analysis and follow-through. The board's role in risk management should follow this guidance: Stay focused on fiduciary responsibilities and strategic direction, and rely on the administration for the data, reports, plans, and execution.

---

[6] For additional resources from AGB, see Pelletier, Stephen G. "High-Performing Committees: What Makes Them Work?" *Trusteeship*, May/June 2012.

Exhibit 9: **Sample Assignment of Risks to Board Committees**

Board of Trustees Committee Oversight of Risks Report

Financial Stewardship

Risk Area	Responsible Management	Responsible Committee
Internal Controls	• University Controller	Audit
Finance Management	• Vice President for Finance and CFO	Finance
Budget Management	• Vice President for Planning and Budget	Finance
Endowment Management	• Chief Investment Officer • Vice President for Alumni Affairs and Development	Investment
Medical Billing Compliance	• Provost for Medical Affairs (Medical College) • Associate Dean, Billing Compliance (Medical College)	Audit
Financial Fraud	• University Auditor	Audit
Subsidiaries & Affiliates	• Subsidiary Management and Board of Directors • Vice President for Finance and CFO • Executive Vice Provost for Administration and Finance (Medical College)	Executive

Safety and Security

Patient Safety & Medical Malpractice	• Vice President for Student and Academic Services • Executive Director Health Services • Chief Medical Officer Physician Organization • Executive Vice Provost for Administration and Finance (Medical College)	Executive
Environmental Health & Safety	• Vice President for Human Resources • Senior Director Risk Management and Insurance (Medical Center)	Executive
Campus Crime & Code of Conduct Violation	• Chief Cornell Police • Judicial Administrator	Student Life
International Programs	• Vice Provost for International Relations • Senior Executive Vice Dean • Executive Vice Provost for Administration and Finance (Medical College)	Executive
IT Security & Systems Recovery	• Chief Information Officer and Vice President • Chief Information Officer (Medical College)	Audit

Research Programs

Risk Area	Responsible Management	Responsible Committee
Protection of Research Subjects	• Senior Vice Provost for Research • Senior Executive Vice Dean (Medical College)	Audit
Integrity of Research Results	• Senior Vice Provost for Research • Dean of Faculty • Senior Executive Vice Dean (Medical College)	Audit
Allocation of Employees' Effort	• Senior Vice Provost for Research • Vice President Finance and CFO • Senior Executive Vice Dean (Medical College)	Audit
Research-Related Conflicts of Interest	• Senior Vice Provost for Research • Dean of Faculty • Deans • Senior Executive Vice Dean (Medical College)	Audit
Care of Animals	• Senior Vice Provost for Research • Senior Executive Vice Dean (Medical College)	Audit

Employment Issues

Risk Area	Responsible Management	Responsible Committee
Abuse of Authority	• Vice President for Human Resources • Senior Director Human Resources (Medical College)	Executive
Professional Misconduct	• Dean of Faculty • Vice President for Human Resources • Senior Director Human Resources (Medical College)	Executive
Governance-Related Conflicts of Interest	• University Counsel and Secretary of the Corporation	Executive
Discrimination	• Vice President for Human Resources • Senior Director Human Resources (Medical College)	Executive
Sexual Harassment	• Vice President for Human Resources • Senior Director Human Resources (Medical College)	Executive

Ancillary Activities

Risk Area	Responsible Management	Responsible Committee
Athletics Controversies	• Vice President for Student and Academic Services • Director of Athletics and Physical Education	Student Life
Student Organizations, Fraternities & Sororities	• Vice President for Student and Academic Services • Dean of Students	Student Life

Corporate Officers = President, Provost, Provost for Medical Affairs, Vice President for Finance and CFO, University Counsel and Secretary of the Corporation

Adapted from Cornell University. Reprinted with permission.

and interest in growing a stronger presence in international programs may prompt a task force of members of the student affairs, academic affairs, and finance committees to study the multifaceted risk and report to the respective committees. If a task force or the executive committee is appointed, it is important that they provide the full board an analysis and review of these risks.

A Word About the Audit Committee

Boards are often tempted to assign responsibility for risk management to the audit committee alone, with a sigh of relief that now *someone* will be responsible for risk and the rest of the board can rest easy. The audit committee does a great job, the thinking goes, with reviewing the financial statements, checking on insurance coverage, meeting with the internal audit manager[7] (if the institution is large enough to have this function), and monitoring compliance issues—so why not give the audit committee the challenging job of overseeing institutional risk management? While perhaps neat and tidy, and similar to how many corporate boards function, heed caution. It can be argued that numerous areas of higher education operate like a business and should be run as such. Yet this argument falls short in helping the institution understand, prepare for, and respond to the risks and opportunities that it faces. The purpose of a commercial business is to make money. Having risk management the responsibility of the audit or finance committee aligns the financial priority of the business with its financial risks. But, the business of higher education is teaching, learning, research, and service. While financial aspects are important—after all, there is no mission without margin—viewing risk management solely through the prism of finances creates a narrow lens through which the institution's strategic mission is not fully considered.

When overseeing cross-functional risk issues, each group assigned (board committee, the full board, a task force) should:

1. Review the risks identified by the senior administration. *(See Chapter 2, Step 1.)*

---

[7] For additional resources from AGB, see Vekich, Michael and Daniel Coborn. "Accountability is a Calculated Effort." *Trusteeship*, September/October 2004.

2. Ask questions on the process and scope of the risk identification process. *(See Part II.)*

3. Discuss and agree on the institution's risk tolerance for risks brought forward to the committees.

4. Review the risk mitigation plans or treatment proposed by the administration.

5. Regularly monitor the administration's identification, assessment, and mitigation plans.

Which committee should oversee strategic, yet risky, new initiatives?

Campus professionals and audit committee members in academic institutions and foundations where the board's risk management responsibilities reside in the audit or finance committee report some common themes and concerns. Most important is that institutions operating this way tend to monetize risks and may fail to address the strategic, reputational, and mission risks as effectively as they should.

Proposal: The alumni office and the career services staff proposed that the university consider offering additional courses to keep former students current in their field and connected to campus. The administration believed that the institution remained on the top of alumni minds when it came to seeking professional development. An online learning program to serve alumni was proposed.

Dilemma: Administrators felt hard pressed to handle an initiative to launch such an online learning program to reach alumni. Yet the project offered the potential to both add to the bottom line and support the mission.

Decision: Assigning this initiative (and risks) to the academic affairs committee, rather than the audit committee, created deeper understanding and engagement among board members of the institution's programs and this initiative's relationship to other institutional priorities.

Risk Questions for the Academic Affairs Committee:

1. Has a formal market study been completed measuring interest in the idea and alternative options available to alumni?

2. Has the institution discussed partnering with other institutions or for-profit firms to develop online alumni courses?

3. Has legal counsel reviewed interstate regulations in offering online courses and other consumer-focused regulations?

Lesson: If the strategic direction of a new program or initiative is evaluated by a particular board committee, the attendant risks should reside with the same committee.

Part II
THE BOARD AND
BOARD COMMITTEES

As outlined in Part I: Fundamentals of Risk Management, the enterprise risk management (ERM) process, led by senior administrators, identifies the top risks the institution faces. Part II focuses on strategic, board leadership, finance, and operational risks. The purpose of these chapters is to provide background information on a variety of risk areas prevalent in higher education and to enable the full board and specific board committees to better explore these risks. The risks that are raised in the following chapters closely track the scope of the board and specific committees.

Not all of these risks will be on the risk register of every institution. Some may have been omitted by the senior administration when compiling the risk register, and others may not be applicable. The complexities of large research universities present different risks than small liberal arts colleges do. Multi-campus public university systems face different risks than community colleges. Depending on their structure and scope, institutionally related foundations face their own unique set of risks, some of which may echo those identified here.

The board and its committees can use the conversation-starting questions in the following chapters to identify risks the administration may have omitted in its review and to support their understanding of the risk mitigation plans. But, because many aspects of the higher education environment are changing at breakneck speed, neither the risks nor the questions are complete or comprehensive. Board members have an obligation to stay current on emerging issues and ask probing questions on those and other issues.

4

STRATEGIC RISKS

Standing committees have an important role in working with the senior administration to assess the risks and responses facing the institution. Some risks do not fit neatly within the charter and purview of the standing committees and can be the work of the full board. While some of these risks could be addressed by the executive committee, for reasons addressed in AGB's *Effective Committee Series: The Executive Committee,* the full board—sometimes facilitated through ad hoc committees or task forces—is the ideal place for discussion of risks that cross institutional boundaries.

Risks that ultimately fall under the purview of the full board include:

- Strategic planning;
- Crisis response and business continuity;
- Reputation and brand;
- Community relations; and
- Information technology.

Strategic Planning

To start the dialogue, the full board should ask:

- **Metrics.** Has the institution identified the appropriate metrics and tracking tools, beyond financial ratios, to provide timely and accurate reports on performance against its plans?
- **Data quality.** Does the board have confidence in the quality of the data and ongoing metrics and reports?

- **New initiatives.** Is a sound business plan in place for evaluating new programs, regulatory requirements, and other special initiatives? Do these plans take into account income and expense assumptions and identify key risk factors?

The power and value of a strategic plan, which articulates the institution's aspirations and priorities, should not be underestimated. Discussions with accrediting commissions reveal that an institution's planning process is an important criterion, explicitly in specific standards and implicitly in the tone and focus of the accreditation process. While the accreditation process primarily focuses on academic quality, it also assesses whether the institution will continue to be in business for the next five to ten years and graduate students as promised. A well-constructed, thoroughly-tested, and clearly-displayed strategic plan helps to answer that question.

> **"Planning is the one area that generates major governance problems, most often manifested as the absence of planning."**
>
> — Sylvia Manning, president, Higher Learning Commission

"Does the institution adequately plan *and* monitor its performance against that plan?" is a pervasive question throughout all accreditation reviews and an important risk management question for boards to ask of senior leadership. Ralph Wolff, president of the Western Association of Schools and Colleges, notes that institutions are called upon to assess their "changing ecology," which includes demographics, competition, external funding, and elasticity of demand for education, among other factors. In turn, boards must assess the rigor and thoroughness of the institution's interpretation of and response to this changing ecology.

Plans are just that, plans. As circumstances change, the strategic plan and institutional priorities may also evolve. From its vantage point, the board should encourage the institution to identify programs and services that can be phased out or eliminated to make room for new initiatives. New programs and partnerships are often incorporated into a strategic plan, and the board should insist that an ERM analysis be completed for major new programs and ventures.[8]

---

[8] For additional resources from AGB, see:
- Chabotar, Kent John. *Strategic Finance: Planning and Budgeting for Boards, Chief Executives, and Finance Officers*, 2006.
- MacTaggart, Terrence. *Leading Change: How Boards and Presidents Build Exceptional Academic Institutions,* 2011.

Crisis Response and Business Continuity

To start the dialogue, the board may ask:

- **Crisis response plan.** Does the campus have a crisis response plan, and is it regularly tested and revised? Does it include a communications plan?

- **Board communications.** Do board members understand their collective and individual roles in a crisis? Are procedures in place to keep the board members informed during a crisis?

- **Presidential contingency plan.** Is a plan in place to respond if a crisis is directed at the president?

- **Data recovery.** Does the crisis response plan include an evaluation of technology needs to support recovery of data and restoration of all services? Does it include evaluation of campus research to support protection and recovery?

Hazing, alcohol abuse, sports scandals, sexual assault, shootings, high-profile tenure decisions, and board member misbehavior begin the list of high-profile campus crises that plague higher education institutions. But external events beyond the institution, such as a flood, earthquake, or hurricane, can also become a crisis.[9] Left unheeded, societal trends of shifting demographics, declining state support, and competition from new education providers can also become institutional crises. Like the comfortable frog that sits in the water as it slowly reaches a boil, a trend is not a crisis, until it is.

Campus leaders should recognize that crises are not predictable but are inevitable. A crisis is an unplanned event that has the potential to endanger community members or the institution's facilities or reputation. It is easy for institutional leaders to think that they are immune from the headline-grabbing, mission-weakening crises that afflict other campuses, but history proves otherwise. Large and small, ru-

---

[9] For additional resources from AGB, see:
- Bourbon, Julie. "University of Iowa Flooding: The Expected and the Unexpected." *Trusteeship*, September/October 2008.
- Chynoweth, Lyn Trodahl. "Creating Solutions in Times of Crisis." *Trusteeship*, November/December 2011.
- White, Lawrence. "Governing During an Institutional Crisis: 10 Fundamental Principles." *Trusteeship*, January/February 2012

ral, suburban and urban, crises do not discriminate. A "Cool Head, Warm Heart"[SM] philosophy is a principled approach for responding to a crisis. In short, it includes responding to families and the community in a caring manner while adhering to established policies and practices that limit liability and speed recovery.

Many academic institutions spend a disproportional amount of time identifying the risks that could derail or delay their plans and mission. Similarly, institutions spend significant time and energy developing crisis response plans but very little time testing the plan. If this is the case, boards should encourage flipping the planning and practicing equation. *(See page 10, "Insight: Invert the 80/20 rule.")* While the institution cannot predict what the crisis will be or when it will occur, the leadership should practice how to respond to a wide range of possible risks. Remembering that the nature of a crisis means that nothing goes as planned, practice— through a table-top drill or mock exercise involving community participants when possible—ensures that the campus will be ready for the inevitable.

The complexity and intensity of some of the most prominent scandals to hit higher education require expertise in response that is well beyond any campus.[10] John Burness, visiting professor of public policy at Duke University, notes, "No campus is prepared for the media spotlight that accompanies a crisis of the size and scope that occurred at Duke University or Penn State. Even the most experienced campus public relations staff need outside help." The need for immediate responses—via multiple channels—and the viral potential of events and any additional missteps calls for specialized expertise beyond the experience and talent of internal staff. Having an external communications firm or consultant familiar with the institution, its culture, and its circumstances can provide much-needed additional support for managing the messages in the midst of a crisis.

Insight: Know where the crisis management "A team" resides

In hindsight, campus leaders who have lived through headline-grabbing events often acknowledge that stumbles were made immediately after the crisis while the campus team tried to respond *and* hire a public relations firm with relevant higher education experience—all within hours after the crisis hit. One president commented, "We tried to respond ourselves to the crisis for the first 24 hours, got the B team from a PR firm for the next 36 hours, and then finally identified the A team. But we were three days into the crisis with much damage done before we were truly ready to respond."

---

[10] For additional resources from AGB, see "When Governance Goes Awry: What are the Takeaways?" *Trusteeship*, September/October 2012.

There is a role for a board before and during a crisis but, unless the crisis is focused on the president directly, the board's role is limited to ensuring that a plan is in place, requiring that it be regularly tested, and supporting the president and senior administrative team.

Reputation and Brand

To start the dialogue, the full board may ask administrators:

- **Reputation.** Does the institution know what components of its reputation are the most valuable?
- **Recovery strategy.** Does the institution have a reputation recovery strategy that moves beyond a crisis response or business continuity plan?
- **Rebranding.** If there is a strategy to rebrand the institution, does the campus community, including alumni, support the aspirational brand?
- **Core beliefs.** Does the branding strategy truly represent the mission, values, and core beliefs of the institution?
- **Brand audit.** Has an institutional brand audit (done either with internal or external experts) been completed within the last five years to ensure clarity and consistency of the brand?

As Warren Buffett famously advised, "It takes 20 years to build a reputation and five minutes to ruin it. If you think about that, you'll do things differently." To paraphrase, institutions spend generations building a reputation that can be tarnished in a very short time. As fiduciaries of an institution of higher education, board members protect its financial, physical, human, and cyber assets, which cumulatively comprise the institution's reputation. Ultimately most of the risk management actions at the board level are focused on preserving the treasured reputation.

Although many in higher education may have been slow to embrace brand management, most institutions now recognize it is an integral part of a strategic plan and risk management strategy. Quantifying what happens to an institution if the brand and reputation are damaged is a challenge. But recognizing that every brand is vulnerable is an important first step.

To analyze this issue from a different perspective, ask: What are the costs or consequences if our institution's reputation is damaged? Answers may include: The capital campaign does not reach its goal in the stated time period; the institution's bond rating is downgraded, increasing the cost of borrowing; star faculty decide to accept competing job offers; and/or highly ranked students decide to study elsewhere. An instructive exercise for board members and administrators is to discuss and come to agreement on the potential consequences of a diminished reputation. This then makes the case for protecting the institution's reputation and developing (and implementing) recovery plans. While institutions can buy adequate insurance to cover some specific risks, insurance does not cover reputational losses, which can greatly overwhelm insured losses.

Community Relations

To start the dialogue, the board may ask administrators:

- **Community impact.** Does the institution provide a clear and current description of the economic and social benefits the institution's programs bring to the community?
- **Community engagement.** Are multiple levels and individuals within the administration involved in community activities and programs? Are these involvements included in the description of economic and social benefits report?
- **Communications.** Are channels of communication open between campus planning activities and local neighbors and planning commissions?

Community relations, often referred to as town/gown relations, are as old as campuses themselves. Wherever it is located, each campus exists as part of a larger community, be it urban, suburban, or rural. And, towns and cities develop around institutions of higher education. This symbiotic relationship can carry risks for colleges and universities when not given the appropriate thought and attention. Campuses bring significant economic benefits to their communities and, often, added costs for emergency response and event management. Because they may not pay corporate, real estate, and other taxes, hosting a college or university may also be seen as reducing tax revenue for the municipality.

Especially for independent colleges and universities, economic pressures on local jurisdictions have re-opened issues related to tax-exempt status and "in lieu of taxes" payments for many municipalities. Some of the ways that academic institutions support their surrounding communities are by conducting research on economic development and incubating small businesses. They also bring additional revenues through tourism and student, faculty, and staff spending in the community. These efforts serve as a strong counter-argument to increasing calls for tax or in-lieu-of-tax payments.

Developing and implementing a strong, cohesive community relations program is the administration's responsibility, but the board has a role in supporting community outreach and engagement initiatives and asking questions that reflect the importance of the relationship. To preempt views by some community and elected officials that the institution is a resource drain rather than a vibrant part of the local economy, boards can encourage the institution to take a strategic and active role in working with business leaders to find ways to support regional and state economic development. Institutions can identify opportunities that will best leverage campus resources, including faculty subject matter experts, facilities, and students to support economic development efforts of the community. Boards can ensure that the proposed initiatives support the institution's strategic plan. Local board members, in particular, can play an important role in communicating and advocating on the institution's behalf.

Information Technology

To start the dialogue, the full board may ask administrators:

- **IT strategy**. Does the institution have an information technology strategy? Does it reflect the institution's core values and strategic plan?
- **Protection.** Do agreements with partners properly protect intellectual property rights and other institutional values (such as privacy and non-discrimination)?
- **Privacy.** Does IT regularly assess changes in privacy and other federal and state compliance areas?
- **Security.** Does the institution perform regular IT security risk assessments and report findings to the board?

- **Missed opportunities.** Is the institution taking enough risk with its IT strategies? Are there opportunities to enhance the educational experience that have not been considered?

Over the past 20 years, information technology (IT) evolved from being an operational support function for financial reporting and student records to becoming an integral part of teaching, research, and service. Data and cyber assets should be counted as one of four assets (human, facilities, financial and cyber) under the board's fiduciary responsibilities for institutional assets. The risks of loss or diminution of any of these assets is an important part of the institution's risk management strategy.

Institutions benefit from having IT experts serve on their boards. They bring a wealth of experience and knowledge of trends in a rapidly changing industry. While there are many similarities between IT issues in higher education and commercial businesses, the differences are also substantial, and boards need to recognize the differences as well as the commonalities. The culture of higher education is one of transparency, openness, and collaboration. Businesses can operate secure and closed systems, while colleges, universities, and foundations serve broad communities from students, alumni, and donors to researchers and faculty. Small to midsized academic institutions have correspondingly smaller staff that are generalists without the level of specialization or access to the top vendors of large corporate (and some large research university) IT departments. Boards that understand these contexts and issues of scale are best positioned to help their institutions identify, assess, and mitigate IT risk.[11]

Data Collection, Integrity, and Analysis

Within the IT function, the emphasis on decision making is shifting from technology to information. IT discussions in higher education now include not just hardware and software considerations but also more intangible issues, such as privacy and instructional learning methodology. The emerging world of data analytics sup-

---

[11] For an additional report from AGB, see Pelletier, Stephen G. and Richard A. Skinner. "Technology in Context: 10 Considerations for Governing Boards of Colleges and Universities," 2010.

ports academic missions and also increases institutional risks. The trend toward collecting and analyzing information on potential students, current students, and alumni offers tremendous opportunities and significant risks. Identifying what data to collect, how they should be analyzed, what privacy and transparency policies should be in place, and whether the campus is prepared to use the analysis are the risks and opportunities of the new frontier of data analytics. The board should confirm that the institution has a privacy policy on the collection and use of such data and that it is made readily available.

Computer System and Data Security

Computer system and data security pose a prominent risk for institutions of higher education. The nature of open networks, extensive systems, "creative" users, and sensitive data creates a temptation for mischievous and/or criminal actions. Recovery, legal advice, and forensics work required to respond to a data breach are extremely expensive. For IT risks, the 80/20 rule should allocate 80 percent of resources to developing and testing IT security systems (including on-campus and mobile computing) and 20 percent of resources to responding to the significantly reduced risk of a major breach. The board should ensure that policies are established and updated periodically, that testing is regularly conducted and reviewed, and that appropriate resources are invested in the security of computer systems and data.

Insight: Data analytics support missions but raise privacy and data security risks

The power of data analytics that is sweeping the business world has the potential to change student health services, academic advising, and alumni relations. Data on a student's class attendance, number of meals eaten in the dining hall, library visits, and attendance at sporting events are collected on many campuses. Such data can be analyzed and, using predictive modeling techniques, campus administrators could potentially identify students with substance abuse problems, students most likely to drop out, and/or those likely to become loyal and generous alumni. Questions that the board should ask and that should be answered include:

- Does the institution have a data analytics strategy?
- Is the institution collecting the right data?
- Is the institution willing to act on the data for the good of the institution?
- What is the institution's policy on privacy of data?

5

BOARD GOVERNANCE RISKS

Executive Committee

Most boards of independent institutions and related foundations have an executive committee, as do a growing number of public institutions and systems boards. The principal purpose of an executive committee is to act on behalf of the board, as needed, between meetings and to assume specific responsibilities not otherwise assigned to standing or ad hoc committees. As described in *The Executive Committee*, the committee's work generally falls into five broad categories:

1. Significant matters dictated by the calendar of events that cannot wait for a board meeting;

2. Processes that the committee has specifically been charged with facilitating, such as presidential compensation or oversight of strategic planning;

3. Matters referred to the committee by the board, chair, or president for study and possible resolution, such as community relations or public policy;

4. Issues generated by the committee itself or that intersect with the work of other committees and require cross-functional coordination, such as risk assessment or brand management; and

5. Routine or relatively inconsequential matters requiring pro forma action by the committee to conserve the board's time, such as approving board meeting agendas.[12]

---

[12] For additional resources from AGB, see Legon, Richard D. *The Executive Committee* (Effective Committee Series), 2012.

"Executive committees that shift into activities reserved exclusively for the full board, and fail to communicate to the board, risk alienating the board and eroding a culture of strong governance essential to a strong and effective board. An executive committee that understands its appropriate role and has a transparent discussion of these questions will turn a risky situation into a force of positive governance."

—Richard Legon, AGB president, in *The Executive Committee*

The executive committee can play a role in helping the audit committee identify gaps in the board's risk management oversight. If the committee includes chairs of other standing committees and rotating at-large members, the executive committee can assess gaps in the risk identification work done by the senior administration and standing committees. Standing committees of the board are best positioned to evaluate the risk identified by the senior administration specifically related to their respective committee charges. However, some risks to an institution (such as those described in Chapter 4) may overlap several committees or fall outside the purview of specific committees. In those instances, the executive committee may lead the board in examining these risks and coordinating input from multiple committees.

In addition, an executive committee usually has responsibility for two areas of risk: 1) its own committee scope and 2) talent management and succession planning.

Executive Committee Scope

To start the dialogue, executive committee members should ask themselves:

1. **Boundaries.** Are we overstepping the boundaries delineated in the bylaws?
2. **Information sharing.** What information can and should we share with the full board, and when?
3. **Agenda.** Is the board chair fully engaged in setting the executive committee's agenda?
4. **Chair responsibility.** Does the chair assume responsibility for informing other board members of the executive committee's agenda, priorities, and current work?

The greatest risk the executive committee will encounter, as a committee, is an expansion of its activities and authority, which compromises the engagement and authority of the full board. The executive committee should resist the temptation to take on risk assessment activities. Instead, when possible, it should delegate them to other standing or ad hoc committees.

Talent Management and Succession Planning

To start the dialogue, executive committee members should ask:

- **Talent management.** Does the institution have appropriate plans in place to attract and retain senior administrators and faculty?

Case in Point: Managing cross-functional gaps in risk management

In reviewing the work of the multiple committees, the executive committee is well positioned to identify gaps of both risk and opportunities that may not otherwise be uncovered. With the benefit of such a discussion by the executive committee, the committees and administration can then bring a more thoughtful analysis to the full board for consideration.

Consider this example. A university recognized the importance of increasing its online learning presence and made it a strategic priority. But, the administration also knew that its technology readiness was a challenge. So, the executive committee tasked other standing committees with examining different aspects of this issue, as follows:

Standing Committee	Risks of increasing online learning presence
Student Affairs	Diverse student body arriving on campus with disparity of devices prompts consideration of including technology funding in financial aid packages.
Academic Affairs	Investments are needed in training and equipment for faculty to offer online and hybrid courses. Review compliance with Americans with Disabilities Act.
Finance Committee	Budgeted full-time enrollments may decline as more students bring credits from nationally available online courses to institution; mobile computing portals need significant upgrades and budget support.
Full Board	Security issues need to be addressed to accommodate broader usage.

Conclusion: A discussion of these risks revealed the opportunity to partner with other colleges and universities through a consortium to share development costs for courses, which then could be offered to students from all institutions.

- **Succession.** Are succession plans in place for replacing senior administrators in the event of an emergency and/or over a longer time period?
- **President evaluation.** Is a thorough annual evaluation process in place for the president's performance?
- **Executive compensation.** Are the results of the president's evaluation and compensation package shared with the full board?
- **Diversity.** Does the institution promote a climate that supports women and minorities and encourages their professional development?

Higher education is a people business. More than 65 percent of most institutions' operating budgets are compensation expenses. It follows that human resources problems and employment lawsuits are also one of the most frequent (and expensive) liability risks institutions encounter. While the full board's responsibility is hiring, evaluating, and dismissing the president, supporting the president's efforts to attract and retain high-caliber senior administrators is important to the institution's long-term health and vitality. Supporting the administration's development and implementation of training for all faculty and staff, with a special emphasis on supervisors, is also an important role for the executive committee.

The financial pressures and complexity of academic institutions impose new challenges on the ability to attract and retain high-quality, engaged campus administrators and leaders. The executive committee may also serve as the compensation committee, meeting with an external compensation expert to assess comparability of the president's compensation, soliciting ongoing feedback on the president's performance, and, through the board chair, delivering the annual performance review and compensation decisions to the president and the full board.[13]

---

[13] For additional resources from AGB, see:
- Atwell, Richard. *Presidential Compensation in Higher Education*, 2008.
- MacTaggart, Terrence. "How Presidential Evaluations Must Change." *Trusteeship*, January/February 2012).
- Morrill, Richard L. "Assessing Presidential Effectiveness." *Trusteeship*, January/February 2010.
- Morrill, Richard L. *Assessing Presidential Effectiveness: A Guide for College and University Boards*, 2010.
- Roady, Celia. "Compensation Chemistry." *Trusteeship*, January/February 2008.

Governance Committee

The governance committee (sometimes known as the committee on trustees or the nominating committee) serves a unique role in board performance and in setting the tone for risk management. The risks that fall under the purview of the governance committee include:

- Board recruitment and development;
- Board performance assessment;
- Conflict of interest and code of conduct oversight; and
- Board policies and procedures, including institutional bylaws.

This is not a complete list; new risks will emerge over time at each institution. But, governance committees should understand that these board issues can pose risks to the institution. Each governance committee should identify risks related to board functioning and then ensure that mitigation plans are developed and followed.

Board Recruitment and Development

To start the dialogue, the governance committee should ask itself:

- **Board composition needs.** Does the committee maintain a thorough list of skills, experience, and perspectives needed to enhance the board and use this list to identify candidates?
- **Board expectations.** Does the committee maintain and share with prospective nominees a clear description of the role and responsibilities of board members, including attendance and gift expectations?
- **Orientation and mentoring.** Does the board hold comprehensive orientation and assign mentors to new board members?
- **Ongoing board education.** Does the committee identify strengths and areas of current board knowledge and, with the president and board professional, identify needed board education and training programs in response?

In the current environment, board recruitment and development includes concerns that can pose risks for boards of colleges, universities, systems, and foundations.

Those risk factors include board member independence (and conflicts of interest), board member attendance, board knowledge and information sharing, and full board participation in decision making.

Some boards, most often those of independent colleges and universities and of related foundations, are self-perpetuating and not dependent on elections or appointment of members. These boards have the responsibility to identify and cultivate a strong and engaged board. Developing clear criteria to identify and cultivate prospective board members should be a high priority for the governance committee. In practice, this means developing a matrix of skills and experience needed and recognizing special talents and expertise that may enhance the ability of the board to meet its duties. For example, if the institution is trying to achieve a more national presence, the governance committee should identify candidates from a geographically diverse area.

Whether the board is self-perpetuating, elected, or appointed, comprehensive board orientation and mentorship programs encourage a quick assimilation of the board's culture. An exemplary orientation process includes a balance between education on fiduciary responsibilities and an understanding of how the institution works. When combined with a mentoring program, a strong orientation creates a safe space for new board members to ask questions and existing board members to offer private guidance on the roles and responsibilities of board members.

Orientation should be carried through into ongoing board education, and time should be allotted at regular board meetings to examine the big issues affecting higher education, the institution, and the board's work. Not properly onboarding and educating board members can hinder the effectiveness of the board. New, and sometimes returning, board members may distract the board by moving into territory that is not the purview of the board or by focusing on less relevant issues at the expense of institutional priorities.[14]

---

[14] For additional resources from AGB, see:

- Bahls, Steven C. "Board Complacency and the Experienced President." *Trusteeship*, January/February 2011.
- MacTaggart, Terrence J. "The Risks of Trustee 'Managerialism.'" *Trusteeship*, January/February 2007.
- Novak, Richard. "State Policies and Practices to Improve Board Governance." *Trusteeship*, September/October 2012.
- Wilson, E.B. and Jim Lanier. *Governance Committee* (Effective Committee Series), 2013.

Board Performance Assessments

To start the dialogue, the governance committee should ask itself:

- **Board and committee evaluations.** Are board evaluations and committee evaluations completed and reviewed by the governance committee? How often?
- **Board member self-assessments.** Are individual board member self-assessments completed and reviewed by the governance committee?
- **Board strengths and weaknesses.** Does the committee identify strengths and areas for development of the board and develop appropriate board education activities in response?

Regular board assessments—of the full board, committees, and individuals—provide the governance committee with insights on board engagement, satisfaction, and effectiveness. Boards that fail to regularly assess individual members, committees, and full board performance increase the risk of perpetuating ineffective governance processes, ongoing conflicts, or dysfunctional deliberations. A well-functioning board cannot eliminate institutional risks, but it can increase the odds that they will be identified and managed appropriately. An institution is only as good as its board. Strong boards are more able to attract, retain, and support a strong president. And, they help the institution fulfill its mission and implement its plans.

Board assessments are important undertakings for the governance committee because they enable it to identify and address potential problems. The governance committee should create opportunities for board members to evaluate their contribution to the board and the institution, and for board committees [15] and the full board to evaluate their work and adherence to their respective charters. Well-tested assessment instruments exist for assessing individual, committee, and board performance. Committee and board assessments should be done periodically—best practice is every three years—and reviewed by the governance committee. Individual board member self-assessments should be done prior to reappointment to the board.

---

[15] For additional resources from AGB, see Pelletier, Stephen G. "High-Performing Committees: What Makes Them Work?" *Trusteeship*, May/June 2012.

Conflicts of Interest and Code of Conduct

To start the dialogue, the governance committee should ask:

- **Conflicts of interest**. Does the board have a conflict of interest policy? Does it require annual disclosure? Is it followed consistently?
- **Code of conduct.** Does the institution have a code of conduct? Do board members adhere to it?

All board members must understand and follow the institution's conflict of interest policy and code of conduct; nonadherence presents particular risks to the institution. Oversight and enforcement of these policies—as they relate to the board—often fall under the jurisdiction of the governance committee (or sometimes the executive or audit committee).

A conflict of interest policy spells out the responsibility of board members to act in an unbiased manner that is in the best interests of the institution without regard to personal interest or gain *(see Exhibit 10)*. The policy should prescribe, to board members and officers, the institution's commitment to avoid both actual conflicts of interests and the appearance of such conflicts. Because of the transactional nature of matters that come before the investment and facilities committees, special attention should be paid to potential or perceived conflicts with their members.

Opinions differ on whether a board (or committee) member may have any business relationship with an institution. The institution, through the governance committee and the board, should decide what, if any, business relationships can exist and identify when compelling reasons or extraordinary circumstances may allow for certain business relationships. Regardless, *in all cases*, the business relationship should be fully disclosed to the board. *(See Exhibit 11 for guiding principles from AGB: 2012 Statement on External Influences on Universities and Colleges.)*

Best practice is for all board and committee members (if committees have non-board members serving on them) to complete annual statements disclosing any existing or possible conflicts of interest. The governance committee should review these statements and respond as needed. Periodically, the governance committee should review and recommend for full board approval updated conflict of interest policies for the board, faculty, and administrators. It should also oversee the implementation of the policy and receive reports on its completion.[16]

In addition to a conflict of interest policy, the committee should maintain and annually share a code of conduct policy that clearly articulates expectations of each board member.

Bylaws, Policies, and Procedures

To start the dialogue, the governance committee should ask:

- **Bylaws.** When were the bylaws last reviewed? Do they incorporate any legal or regulatory changes? Do they reflect how the board currently operates?
- **Policies.** Is the board manual current and up-to-date? Do all board members have a copy or electronic access to it?

Bylaws provide a roadmap for good governance. They outline the duties of board members and officers, procedures for holding meetings, elections processes, conflict of interest and indemnification policies, and other essential corporate governance matters. To be effective, they must be current. Bylaws are governed by state law and should be reviewed by legal counsel every five years to ensure that they reflect both changes in laws and significant changes in how the board conducts its business.

The bylaws become very important when something goes wrong, either internally or from an external source. While bylaws might not be regularly referenced by board members, if the institution is involved in a lawsuit, the bylaws become a foundational document for guiding the board through the conflict.[17]

---

[16] For additional resources from AGB, see:
- Dreier, Alexander E. and Martin Michaelson. *A Guide to Updating the Board's Conflict of Interest Policy*, 2006.
- Michaelson, Martin. "How is Your Institution Doing on Conflicts of Interest?" *Trusteeship*, November/December 2007.

[17] For additional resources from AGB, see:
- O'Neil, Robert. *Updating Board Bylaws: A Guide for Colleges and Universities*, 2012
- White, Lawrence. "The Principle of Indemnification and Why Trustees Should Care About It." *Trusteeship*, March/April 2012.

The board's policies and procedures, which clarify the components and implementation of its legal fiduciary obligations, are also the responsibility of the governance committee. More specifically, a policy manual or handbook should be in place to guide the work of the board and its committees. The governance com-

---

Exhibit 10: **AGB Conflict of Interest Principles**

1. Each board must bear ultimate responsibility for the terms and administration of its conflict of interest policy. Although institutional officers, staff, and legal counsel can assist in administration of the policy, boards should be sensitive to the risk that the judgment of such persons may be impaired by their roles relative to the board's.

2. We believe that the following standard properly gauges whether a board member's actual or apparent conflict of interest should be permissible, with or without (as the situation warrants) institutional management of the conflict: (a) If reasonable observers, having knowledge of all the relevant circumstances, would conclude that the board member has an actual or apparent conflict of interest in a matter related to the institution, the board member should have no role for the institution in the matter. (b) If, however, involvement by the board member would bring such compelling benefit to the institution that the board should consider whether to approve involvement, any decision to approve involvement should be subject to carefully defined conditions that assure both propriety and the appearance of propriety.

3. (a) When a board member is barred by actual or apparent conflict of interest from voting on a matter, ordinarily the board member should not participate in or attend board discussion of the matter, even if to do so would be legally permissible. (b) If, however, the board determines that it would significantly serve the interests of the board to have the conflicted board member explain the issue or answer questions, the board, if legally free to do so, may consider whether to invite the board member for that limited purpose. Any resulting invitation should be recorded in the minutes of the meeting.

4. A board should not confine its conflict of interest policy to financial conflicts, but should instead extend that policy to all kinds of interests that may (a) lead a board member to advance an initiative that is incompatible with the board member's fiduciary duty to the institution, or (b) entail steps by the board member to achieve personal gain, or gain to family, friends, or associates, by apparent use of the board member's role at the institution.

Source: AGB Board of Directors' Statement on Conflict of Interest (December 2009)

mittee's role in risk management begins with reviewing board-level policies and procedures (or making sure that they are reviewed by the appropriate committee) on a regular basis to ensure that they are up-to-date and that the board follows them.

5. Board members should be required to disclose promptly all situations that involve actual or apparent conflicts of interest related to the institution as the situations become known to them. To facilitate board members' identification of such conflicts, institutions should take affirmative steps at least annually to inform their board members of major institutional relationships and transactions, so as to maximize awareness of possible conflicts.

6. Board members should be required to disclose not less often than annually interests known by them to entail potential conflicts of interest.

7. At institutions that receive substantial federal research funding, financial thresholds for mandatory disclosure of board members' conflicts of interest should not be higher than the thresholds then in effect that regulate conflicts of interest by faculty engaged in federally sponsored research. Boards of institutions that do not receive substantial federal research funding should take into account the federal sponsorship-related thresholds in determining thresholds for mandatory disclosure of board member conflicts of interest.

8. Interests of a board member's dependent children, and of members of a board member's immediate household, should be disclosed and regulated by the conflict of interest policy applicable to board members in the same manner as are conflicts of the board member.

9. Institutional policy on board member conflicts of interest should extend to the activities of board committees and should apply to all committee members, including those who are not board members.

10. Boards should consider whether to adopt conflict of interest policies that specifically address board members' parallel or "side-by-side" investments in which the institution has a financial interest.

11. Boards should also consider whether to adopt especially rigorous conflict of interest provisions applicable to members of the board investment committee.

12. To the extent that the foregoing recommendations exceed but are not inconsistent with state law requirements applicable to members of public college and public university boards, such boards should voluntarily adopt the recommendations.

For AGB's full statement on Conflicts of Interest, see www.agb.org.

Exhibit 11: AGB Guiding Principles on External Influences on Universities and Colleges

Boards must police themselves in assuring the highest level of ethical behavior among their members, including avoiding any board member assuming the role as an advocate for a special interest in the outcome of a board's decision.

Governing boards must:

1. **Preserve institutional independence and autonomy by:**

   - Keeping the mission as a beacon;

   - Ensuring that philanthropy does not inappropriately influence institutional independence and autonomy or skew academic programs or mission; and

   - Ensuring that institutional policies governing corporate-sponsored research and partnerships with the private sector are clear, up-to-date, and periodically reviewed.

2. **Demonstrate board independence to govern as established in charter, state law, or constitution by:**

   - Ensuring the full board governs as a collective, corporate body taking into consideration the need for individual members to apply their individual consciences and judgments;

   - Individual board members committing to the duties of care, loyalty, and obedience as essential fiduciary responsibilities; and

   - Basing the selection or appointment of board members on merit and their ability to fulfill the responsibilities of the position.

3. **Keep academic freedom central and be the standard bearer for the due-process protection of faculty, staff, and students.**

4. **Assure institutional accountability to the public interest by:**

   - Serving as a bridge to the external community;

   - Informing, advocating, and communicating on behalf of the institution;and

   - Exhibiting exemplary public behavior.

Source: *AGB Statement on External Influences on Universities and Colleges* (2012).
(See full statement at: www.agb.org)

6

FINANCIAL RISKS

Boards are responsible for the future of their institution, which includes financial and strategic oversight; balanced operating budgets and funding for deferred maintenance; prudent investment policies, adequate liquidity, and serviceable long-term debt; and fundraising and advancement efforts. Given the magnitude of these responsibilities, the board relies on several committees to facilitate this work.

Finance Committee

Finance committees provide guidance and oversight to an institution's financial and business operations. They ensure that the institution has a long-term plan that is continually updated and monitors ongoing financial health. The combination of the business experiences of many board members and the intense financial pressures felt by virtually all educational institutions have expanded the role of the finance committee. In addition, financial transactions have increased in complexity, from interest rate swaps used in borrowing money for construction to indirect cost recovery for research to revenue sharing for new educational partnerships. The risks that come under the purview of the finance committee include:

- Budgeting and planning;
- Debt;
- Financial strength; and
- Insurance and risk transfer (if not handled by the audit committee).

Insight: Good risk management links mission and margin

The greatest risk for a board is that the institution does not have the necessary resources to achieve its mission and accomplish its strategic plan. Enter the finance committee and its focus on financial strength and sustainability. Risk management can provide a vital link between mission and margin by helping all those involved understand the risk to mission if the financial resources or reputation are seriously degraded.

This is not a complete list; new risks will emerge over time. And some of these risks may not be relevant to every institution. But a board's finance committee should understand that these areas can pose risk to the institution and use that knowledge to ensure that potential gaps in risk identification are revealed and comprehensive mitigation plans are adhered to. The finance committee should receive annual risk reports from senior administrators that indicate the owner(s) of the top risks and describe progress toward mitigation plans. In turn, with guidance from the finance committee and administrators, the full board should understand and discuss the most significant risks.[18]

Budgeting and Planning

To start the dialogue, the finance committee should ask administrators:

- **Mission.** Do the annual and multiyear budgets reflect the values and mission of the institution?
- **Assumptions.** Are the assumptions used in developing the budget realistic, neither too conservative nor too aggressive?
- **Stress-tests.** Are multiyear plans and assumptions stress-tested to illuminate areas of weaknesses and vulnerability?
- **Transparency.** Is there openness and transparency in the development and dissemination of the budget to the appropriate campus communities?

An institution's strategic and annual plans capture the spirit and vision of an institution's future, and the budget is the *financial translation* of these plans. Plans and budgets require a rigor, focus, and transparency to be effective governance tools. The finance committee has the responsibility to test whether the annual budget reflects the institution's priorities and president's goals. They must periodically

---

[18] For additional resources from AGB, see Stafford, Ingrid S. *The Finance Committee* (Effective Committee Series), 2013.

challenge the institution to identify programs or services that should be eliminated or phased out to make room for new initiatives that better align with current goals.

The finance committee helps make sure that the budgeting process considers both upside and downside risks. Some institutions budget so conservatively that they miss opportunities to make strategic investments in areas that will help the institution over the long term. For example, a new program in the career center could strain current staff resources, but it may help students gain meaningful employment, which contributes to long-term goals related to admissions.

Finance committees also have to focus on a constellation of competing forces: net tuition revenue, the quality of the education, and student expectations. Setting annual tuition rates is one of the most difficult functions of a finance committee because it requires balancing the burden on students, with financial aid and other institutional expenses.[19]

Insight: Stress-test to illuminate areas of vulnerability

An important part of a budgeting process should include stress-testing the plans and projections. The finance committee might ask, for example, what if enrollment is 15 percent less? What if annual gifts decline by 20 percent? What if faculty members retire at a slower (or faster) rate?

Financial Strength

To start the dialogue, the finance committee should ask:

- **Ratios.** Does the institution report appropriate financial ratios for monitoring its financial health and viability?
- **Trends.** What trends do the ratios reveal?
- **The long view.** What is the time horizon for costs and revenue projections presented to the board?

At the foundation of a board's responsibility is financial sustainability and protection of the institution's assets. The greatest risk to any institution is that essential resources will no longer be available. While this core duty has always been integral to board service, boards and institutions now face a smaller margin for error,

---

[19] For additional resources from AGB, see:
- Chabotar, Kent John. *Strategic Finance: Planning and Budgeting for Boards, Chief Executives, and Finance Officers*, 2006.
- Schwartz, Merrill. "Making Sense of Tuition Prices and College Costs." *Trusteeship*, July/August 2011.

with fewer cash reserves and less institutional flexibility to recover from declines in revenue. Increased debt load, for both institutions and students, declining federal and state support, and a higher education price index—consistently higher than the consumer price index—all increase the risk that institutions will not be able to maintain the financial resources needed to produce a quality education experience.

"Because boards have the ultimate fiduciary responsibility, one would think they would raise serious concerns each time an increase in tuition well above the rate of inflation was brought to them for approval. Trustees should advocate, expect, and demand greater efficiencies and pilot programs that constrain escalating costs without compromising quality."

—Davis Educational Foundation

The global financial crisis significantly weakened the financial condition of America's colleges and universities. Prior to 2008, liquidity was not a major issue for the majority of institutions. But the economic shocks to endowments, sharp declines in state support, and families' inability (or unwillingness) to contribute more to tuition reduced institutional reserves and resilience. Will economic conditions reverse? Will families be willing to absorb tuition increases that are higher than inflation? Will states return to supporting at previous levels? Answer: It is highly unlikely and far too risky for all but the wealthiest and most prestigious institutions to bank on. Colleges and universities that are not highly selective or do not have strong balance sheets are in the riskiest position because they lack the ability to pass on tuition increases, might not have adequate endowments to provide a cushion, and, in many cases, are in a competitive race to add facilities (often using debt), increase services, and discount tuition.

The finance committee can benefit from looking at metrics[20] and early warning signs *(see Exhibit 12)* to examine the relationship between financial health and mission accomplishment. For example, the following ratios, which are part of the composite financial index (CFI), can reveal answers to strategic finance questions:

[20] For additional resources from AGB, see:
- Bacow, Lawrence and Laura Skandera Trombley. "Making Metrics Matter: How to Use Indicators to Govern Effectively." *Trusteeship*, January/February 2011.
- McLaughlin, Gerald W. and Josetta McLaughlin. *The Information Mosaic: Strategic Decision-Making for Universities and Colleges*, 2008.

Exhibit 12: **Warning Signs for Financial Risks**

Your institution might be at risk if:

1. It is not a top-ranked university or college

- Admissions yield has fallen, and it is costing more to attract students
- Median salaries for graduates have been flat over a number of years
- Endowment is in the millions not billions, and a large percentage is restricted

2. Financial statements do not look as strong as they used to

- Debt expense has been increasing far more rapidly than instruction expense
- Property, plant and equipment (PP&E) asset is increasing faster than revenue

- Institution has seen a decline in net tuition revenue
- Tuition represents an increasingly greater percentage of revenue
- Bond rating has gone down
- Institution is having trouble accessing the same level of government funding

3. It has had to take drastic measures

- Institution is consistently hiking tuition to the top end of the range
- Institution has had to lower admissions standards
- Institution has had to cut back on financial aid
- Institution has reduced faculty head count

Source: Denneen, Jeff and Tom Dretler. *The Financially Sustainable University.* Bain & Company in collaboration with Sterling Partners. July 2012.

- **Primary Reserve Ratio.** Are resources sufficient and flexible enough to support the mission?
- **Viability Ratio.** Are debt resources managed strategically to advance the mission?
- **Return on Net Assets Ratio.** Do asset performance and management support the institution's strategic direction?
- **Net Operating Revenues Ratio.** Do operating results indicate the institution is living within available resources?[21]

Debt

To start the dialogue, the finance committee should ask administrators:

- **Debt service.** Can the institution service its debt over the entire term of the commitment? Are all pro forma financials stress-tested?

---

[21] For more information on metrics, see *Strategic Financial Analysis for Higher Education*, published by KPMG, Prager, Sealy & Co., and Attain.)

- **Reserves.** Does the institution have the appropriate controls on the debt service reserve fund to ensure its stability and liquidity?
- **Transparency.** Is there appropriate transparency and communication with rating agencies and bond holders?[22] Does the institution adhere to the standards and rules promulgated by the rating and regulatory agencies?
- **Counterparty risk.** If the institution uses financial interest rate swaps as part of its debt portfolio, does it have a process to regularly monitor the counterparty risk?
- **Covenants.** Does the institution track and regularly report adherence to bond covenants? Is a process established to seek a waiver in a timely manner if covenants have the potential to be breeched?

Since 2000, colleges and universities have acquired significant amounts of debt for operations and facilities. In the future, their ability to borrow may be constrained. A 2012 report by Bain & Company and Sterling Partners notes that long-term debt is increasing at 12 percent per year, and interest payments of higher education institutions are increasing at twice the amount of instructional costs. The report also notes that administrative and student services costs are increasing at a faster rate than instructional costs. Boards need to question whether the college or university is living beyond its means, and the finance committee should take the lead on such conversations.

After the 2008 global financial crisis, credit markets froze and even the very best credit risks could not borrow money on either a short-term or long-term basis. Many college and university projects were delayed or shelved, the cost of financing projects spiked, and bond insurance (used by many academic institutions in lieu of an individual institutional rating) disappeared. Rating agencies and investment bankers think it unlikely that bond insurance will re-emerge to support institutions without strong financial resources.[23]

Prior to 2008, more than 50 percent of the tax-exempt market was supported

---

[22] Some institutions set up an independent website to share information with bondholders. See Stanford University's website at http://bondholder-information.stanford.edu/disclaimer.html.

[23] For additional resources from AGB, see Lapovsky, Lucie. "A Board's Primer on Bond Ratings." *Trusteeship*, July/August 2007.

by bond insurance. Now, weaker institutions' access to debt markets is—and will continue to be—restricted and/or more expensive as these institutions are less able to take advantage of tax-exempt borrowing. In addition to constricted access to borrowing, colleges and universities are finding a heightened interest by banks and bond holders to add covenants to bond and loan contracts that further restrict the flexibility institutions have to operate. Borrowing money to support operations and capital projects is much riskier now than prior to the global financial crisis.

Audit Committee

The audit committee is the institution's first line of defense when considering financial reporting, internal control, compliance, and risk management. This first line of defense on fiduciary matters leads membership on the audit committee to be more technically focused and requires deep subject matter expertise around financial and compliance issues. Some smaller colleges, universities, and foundations combine the responsibilities of the audit committee and finance committee. This is becoming increasingly difficult because of the complexities and scope of both committees. The risks that fall under the purview of the audit committee[24] include:

- External audit and IRS Form 990;
- Compliance and other external reports;
- Accountability policies (conflicts of interest, fraud reporting and whistle-blower protect, and records retention);
- Insurance and risk transfer (can be covered in finance committee); and
- Internal controls and risk management coordination.

External Audit and IRS Form 990

To start the dialogue, audit committees should ask themselves:

- **External auditors.** Does the audit committee annually meet with external auditors, with and without the president and administrators?
- **Areas for special review.** Working with administration and external

---

[24] For additional resources from AGB, see Staisloff, Richard L. *The Audit Committee* (Effective Committee Series), 2011.

auditors, does the audit committee periodically identify areas for special review?

- **Form 990.** For independent institutions and foundations, does the entire board receive and review the annual IRS Form 990?

External, independent annual audits are the first stop for audit committees. The audit committee has the responsibility to thoroughly review and understand the external auditor's presentation, including additional required letters and management reports. As noted in Chapter 3, institutions can engage audit firms that have deep experience in higher education to assist risk identification and assessment or to assess the quality and thoroughness of the institution's internal accounting processes. In addition, external audit firms are increasingly fulfilling the function of internal auditor.

Because independent institutions and related foundations are nonprofit corporations, their entire board must receive the IRS Form 990, which is, in reality, part tax return and part governance checklist. It asks questions about how the institution and board conducts its business. The form is public information and is easily accessible at www.guidestar.org. While the board, or any individual committee, is not required to approve the Form 990, the IRS asks whether the board received it before its submission. Best practice is for the audit committee to use the completed form to review core governance practices and policies outlined in its questions.

The Form 990 also articulates specific disclosure requirements for conflicts of interest for actions and business relationships within the campus community, including family members *(see also Chapter 5, Governance Committee)*. This has implications not just for the board but well beyond it. For example, institutions with a research program should consider developing an institutional conflict of interest statement and process to address ownership and support of commercial products generated from institutionally funded research.[25]

---

[25] For additional resources from AGB, see:
- Hyatt, Thomas K. "Show Me What I'm Looking For: A Trustee's Guide to Reviewing the New IRS Form 990." *Trusteeship*, January/February 2008.
- Loughry, Andrea J. "Stay Alert to Financial Oversight and Risk Assessment on the Audit Trail." *Trusteeship*, November/December 2007.

Compliance and Other External Reports

To start the dialogue, audit committee members should ask administrators:

- **Legal Compliance.** Does the institution have in place an adequate system to monitor and comply with laws, regulations, and reporting requirements?
- **Other Reporting Mechanisms.** Does the institution have in place an adequate system for ensuring that reports to the public and media are accurate?

Higher education is a highly regulated sector with federal and state legislatures continuing to look for ways to monitor and direct activities and outcomes. Although not at the level of financial institutions and utilities, higher education faces a labyrinth of rules and regulations that must be followed. Non-compliance can lead to fines, liabilities, and/or reputational risk. Compliance requirements vary according to the size, complexity, and mission of the institution. However, all institutions must comply with a core set of employment, financial, safety, and environmental regulations. The size and scope of an institution's athletic programs, research agenda, and international programs are key differentiators in compliance obligations. A variety of useful resources are available online.[26]

Compliance is a risk and should be evaluated and responded to using a framework similar to the broader enterprise risk management (ERM) structure. The senior administration is responsible for developing the structure of the compliance program and regularly reporting to the audit committee on the structure of the program and compliance violations that may be reported to federal or state agencies and therefore become public. The audit committee's role in compliance is to ensure the institution has policies and processes in place so that it is both aware of regulations it is required to follow and can effectively meet these obligations. The reality of the sheer number of regulations requires institutions to make informed judg-

---

[26] For additional information, visit these websites:
- From Higher Education Compliance Alliance, http://www.higheredcompliance.org
- From Catholic University, http://counsel.cua.edu/
- From North Carolina State University, http://www.ncsu.edu/general_counsel/legal_topics/compliance/ComplianceReportingCalendar.php
- From Washington and Lee University, http://www.wlu.edu/x38495.xml

ment calls aimed at determining top compliance priorities or those that should be tackled before less-pressing issues. Institutions must focus initially on regulations that have the greatest potential to provide safety. Then, institutions can evaluate compliance through a thoughtful assessment process, analyzing which regulations bring the greatest financial cost for non-compliance and which bring the greatest reputational costs.

Compliance encompasses more than local, state, and federal rules. Inaccurate reporting to NCAA, *US News & World Report,* and other external parties creates reputational risk. False reporting of information during an accreditation review can jeopardize accreditation. While misrepresenting admissions or other data to the external media may not carry the same consequences, fines, and penalties, reputational damage can be significant and processes should be in place to avoid intentional and unintentional misreporting of data. New programs and initiatives bring both new opportunities and new compliance issues. While the appropriate board committee will review the risks associated with a new program, the audit committee should have a process in place to ensure that any new compliance issues are also addressed.

Insight: International programs often entail additional and ongoing vigilance

Entities, including colleges and universities, considering an acquisition or new venture in a foreign country should be attuned to the Foreign Corrupt Practices Act (FCPA). This law attempts to crack down on illegal conduct in other countries when doing business with American businesses and organizations.[27] Audit committees should ask if appropriate due diligence has been undertaken in the business planning of international programs. Will training be done for staff and faculty on the regulations? Has the administration done its due diligence on the foreign business partners involved in the program? Ongoing monitoring of international programs and evolving regulations and enforcement are essential in this rapidly changing area.

[27] For additional information online, see The Transparency Institute (http://www.transparency.org), which monitors and rates countries for bribery and corruption.

Accountability Policies

To start the dialogue, audit committee members should ask administrators:

- **Conflicts of interest.** Does the institution have a clear, well-written conflict of interest policy for board members, faculty, staff, and vendors?
- **Fraud reporting and whistleblower protection.** Are there processes in place that address how to monitor and respond to whistleblowers and other

reports of misconduct or ethics violations?

- **Records retention.** Does the institution have a process to handle digital and physical documents in the event of pending litigation?

Among the countless policies and procedures at institutions of higher education, some rise to the level of board oversight because of federal law and public perception. Several of them—including conflicts of interest, fraud reporting and whistleblower protection, and records retention—garnered renewed attention with the Sarbanes-Oxley Act of 2002, which brought increased scrutiny to corporate governance and board oversight.

The board has two core functions related to addressing conflicts of interest. The first is to ensure that a strong conflict of interest policy exists and is followed by all individual board members. *(See Chapter 5.)* The second is to ensure that the institution has and regularly monitors adherence to a conflict of interest policy that applies to staff, faculty, and vendors; that outlines steps for responding to any conflicts; and that is implemented rigorously and consistently throughout the institution. For example, institutions with a research program should consider developing a conflict of interest statement and process to address ownership and support of commercial products generated from research. Furthermore, for independent institutions and related foundations, the IRS Form 990 articulates specific disclosure requirements for conflicts for transactions and business relationships of the campus community (including family members).

Unfortunately, fraud is a fact of life in for-profit business, nonprofit enterprises, and government entities. A 2012 Association of Certified Fraud Examiners study reports that 6 percent of worldwide fraud occurs in the higher education sector and 7 percent occurs in the health care sector. The report reveals that 58 percent of fraud cases were discovered by tips or during routine reviews by management. Whistleblowers and tip lines reveal not just instances of financial fraud but other misbehavior, such as sexual assault, discrimination, harassment, and conflicts of interest violations. Prevention programs include three parts:

1. Education and awareness;
2. Reporting and intake process; and
3. Investigation of reports.

Depending on the size of the institution and board structure, the audit committee may be involved in fraud reporting. Third-party vendors provide whistleblower hotlines to receive and record anonymous allegations of wrongdoing. While the cost of whistleblower tip lines is relatively modest, other alternatives exist. Smaller institutions may appoint an individual or team (for example, outside legal counsel, audit committee chair, or other responsible individuals) to receive tips via an anonymous email reporting site. At medium-sized institutions, the audit committee chair may receive a report of all tips submitted. At large institutions, the general counsel may submit a summary of the anonymous tips to the audit committee. Although the administration is responsible for developing and implementing a process for investigation, the audit committee should also periodically review that process.

> " One significant provision in Sarbanes-Oxley, applicable to nonprofit and for-profit institutions alike, makes it a felony to take adverse employment action against any person 'for providing to a law-enforcement officer any truthful information relating to the commission or possible commission of any Federal offense.' "
>
> — Lawrence White, vice president and general counsel, University of Delaware[28]

[28] For additional resources from AGB, see White, Lawrence. "The Whys and Wherefores of Whistleblowing." *Trusteeship*, January/February 2012.

In the past, a record retention policy focused on 1) protection against unplanned destruction of records due to flood, fire, or other accident or employee misconduct and 2) the ability to respond to document production for litigation or public records requests. Today, the retaining, discarding, and managing of records is significantly more complex. Electronic discovery has grown to be a significant litigation expense with terabytes of data from networks in the cloud, on home computer hard drives, in voice mail and text messages, and on social media—all possibly subject to legal discovery in a lawsuit. The institution's record retention policies should address the variety of records maintained by the institution, how they are maintained and archived, and the ability to respond promptly to potential lawsuits.[29]

[29] For additional resources from AGB, see:
- White, Lawrence. "Why Do So Many Lawsuits End in Settlement? Check Your E-Mail." *Trusteeship*, September/October 2011.
- Bernard, Pamela J. "Does Your Institution Need a Social-Media Policy?" *Trusteeship*, September/October 2010.
- Bernard, Pamela J. "New Federal Rules Elevate E-mail as a Risk for Boards and Presidents." *Trusteeship*, March/April 2008.

Insurance and Risk Transfer

To start the dialogue, audit committee members should ask senior administrators, typically the chief financial officer and general counsel:

- **Risk transfer.** Does the institution transfer appropriate risks through insurance?
- **Coverage.** Does the audit committee, at least every five years, review a list of insurance coverage purchased, including limitations, deductibles, and scope (for example, branch campuses, construction)?
- **Contracts.** Does the institution have a process to review third-party contracts to ensure they contain appropriate risk transfer, indemnification, and hold harmless terms and conditions?

An institution faces more risks that are uninsurable than are insurable, but purchasing insurance is a viable strategy to reduce exposure to specific losses. Responsibility for insurance and risk transfer often resides in the audit committee, but some institutions assign it to the finance committee, which may be in a better position to understand the financial consequences of insurance decisions.

The audit committee is well-suited to assess the risk appetite of the institution, assessing how much financial risk can be tolerated given the institution's financial health, liquidity, and other obligations. The audit committee is also best positioned to assess the administration's recommendations on how much risk should be shared or transferred either through purchasing insurance coverage or through contracts with third parties. Institutions contract with outside vendors to provide myriad services from food service to child care, and from summer sports camps to foreign campus operations. Each of these contracts presents an opportunity to evaluate the appropriate level of risk for the institution to hold and what to pass on to the third party through a well-written contract.

The audit committee's role in the insurance review is to:

1. **Monitor the quality of insurance companies selected** by the institution, ensuring that the company is financially strong and able to meet its obligations to pay covered claims. This is particularly important for insurance claims that might take many years to resolve. For example, a sexual

molestation allegation against an employee could take an institution 10 to 20 years to conclude.

2. **Evaluate the limits of coverage purchased.** For example, in evaluating adequate property insurance coverage, the board should know whether all campus facilities are covered in the event of a fire, flood, or other event or if the committee is comfortable (as many institutions are) obtaining coverage for "probable maximum loss"—thereby not having full replacement coverage for the entire facilities inventory.

3. **Evaluate the deductible or self-insured retention**, accepting the institution's responsibility to pay this amount prior to the insurance coverage.

These roles focus on articulating (either explicitly or implicitly) the institution's financial risk tolerance for a specific subset of risks it may encounter. While every institution will consider purchasing certain core lines of insurance, the range of coverage increases significantly based on the complexity, size, and location(s) of the institution:

- A small liberal arts college with one campus and no graduate programs might be well served with only core coverage, while a large, comprehensive university with active research and teaching programs throughout the world could purchase upwards of 40 different types of insurance policies. *(See Appendix C).*

- Public institutions located in a state with strong immunities may only purchase liability insurance to cover claims that fall outside the state immunity protections, including violations of federal laws, cases brought against the institution in another state or country, or cases brought in a way to circumvent the immunity laws.

- Some institutions, particularly large universities with medical centers, establish and manage captive insurance companies to handle either large deductibles or self-insured retentions and/or to fund risks that are not well suited for third-party insurance providers.

- Some public institutions participate in state funding pools that manage claims and cover all losses or enforce charge-back mechanisms. Increasingly, however, public higher education systems are exploring ways to separate from state pools in order to provide more specialized insurance coverage and institutional control over claims.

Internal Controls and Risk Management Coordination

The audit committee performs two core functions related to risk management throughout the institution—monitoring internal controls and coordinating board committees' risk management processes. To start the dialogue, audit committee members can ask administrators:

- **Internal audit.** Does the institution have and adhere to stringent internal financial controls?
- **Committee risk reports.** Does the audit committee receive annual reports on risks reviewed by each standing committee and the full board?

The audit committee monitors the adequacy of the risk management process for compliance, internal controls, and other risks specifically assigned to it. The audit committee's role is similar to the oversight role of internal audit. The Institute of Internal Auditors describes the purpose of the internal audit function as "objective assurance and insight on the effectiveness and efficiency of governance, risk management, and internal control processes." To support the integrity and autonomy of the internal audit function, there is often a reporting relationship between the administration's internal audit function and the board's audit committee. This ensures that the policies and procedures approved by the administration and board are followed.

Most large institutions and many medium-sized institutions have internal audit staff that develop, implement, and monitor internal policies and procedures to improve organizational performance and cost efficiencies. Small to medium institutions may not have internal audit functions or their scope and size may be limited. Or, they may outsource internal audit tasks to a firm with special expertise in higher education. If outsourced, the firm should not be the same one that performs the annual external financial audit. It is important for the board to emphasize the need for candor and openness in the risk identification and assessment process completed by senior administrators, who serve as the risk owners.

In addition to reviewing adherence to institutional risk management policies and processes, internal auditors perform oversight of other financial processes within an institution. Coordination between the internal auditors and risk managers on their respective annual agendas and projects can leverage resources, supporting the administration's broad risk management agenda. But, because of the need to separate duties, it is not appropriate for the internal audit department to lead an enterprise risk management (ERM) initiative. However, the internal auditors and other institutional risk managers should participate in ERM, adding expertise and support throughout the review and analysis.

In the same spirit of internal auditors who work across the organization, the board audit committee can perform a vital role in ensuring appropriate risk management engagement and oversight by the full board. The audit committee should gather and monitor the risk management processes of the standing committees and the full board.

Investment Committee

Risks that fall under the purview of the investment committee include:

- Conflicts of interest;
- Investments; and
- Liquidity.

This is not a complete list as new risks emerge over time. Investment committees should understand that these areas in particular can pose risk to the institution, and use that knowledge to ensure that potential gaps in risk identification are revealed and comprehensive mitigation plans are adhered to. Of course, risk management is at the core of every investment portfolio and integral to achieving the goals of an investment policy. Investing is a continual trade-off of risk and reward. Long before enterprise risk management (ERM) and strategic risk management, investment committees understood volatility, beta, standard deviation, counter-party risk, and other risk and reward calculations that comprise the investors' lexicon.

An investment committee also faces other risks linked to its charter and processes. For starters, the investment committee must establish and adhere to an investment policy, articulate the risk appetite, establish asset allocation, and in most instances hire, monitor, and dismiss investment managers. Establishing good policies and processes is extremely important for an investment committee. Some of the greatest risks an investment committee faces include group think and its opposite—allowing one individual or a subset of the investment committee to drive a decision or point of view, subrogating the committee's policies and sidestepping a thorough analysis. Right sizing the committee to between five and eight voting members helps support active participation and attendance at all meetings. The size of the endowment or the institution's budget should not influence the size of the investment committee; rather expertise and experience should determine committee membership (which may include non-board members). Limiting attendance at investment meetings to only voting members can reduce the amount of external influence and sideline quarterbacking that often accompanies guest attendance.[30]

Investment Committee Composition

To start the dialogue, the investment committee should ask administrators:

- **Committee composition.** Do committee members have financial and investment experience? Is the committee the right size?
- **Conflicts of interest.** Are conflict of interest policies governing investment committee members clear? Are they enforced?

The charter and composition of investment committees open the door for challenges to ambiguous conflict of interest policies. Investment committees benefit from access to unique and specialized expertise. To tap into skills and knowledge from the broader alumni or local community, they may include committee members who are not board members. Regardless, board and committee risk management policies,

---

[30] For additional resources from AGB, see:
- Bahlman, David, John Walda, and Verne Sedlacek. "Higher Education Endowments Return." *Trusteeship*, March/April 2012.
- Bass, David. "Spending and Management of Endowments Under UPMIFA," 2010.
- Curry, John R. and Lyn Hutton. "Why Cash Flow Is No Longer for Wimps." *Trusteeship*, September/ October 2012.
- Griswold, John G. "What Should We Know About Investments and Endowments?" *Trusteeship*, January/February 2013.
- Yoder, Jay A. *The Investment Committee* (Effective Committee Series), 2011.
- Yoder, Jay A. *Endowment Management: A Practical Guide*, 2004.

including conflict of interest policies, should extend to *all* committee members.

Opinions differ as to whether the institution should allow investments with a money manager who serves on the investment committee. AGB's publication *The Investment Committee* describes the two approaches: 1) to take advantage of the unique expertise and allow the investment with disclosure or 2) to not allow institutional investments in funds managed by committee members. The investment committee and full board should discuss the advantages and risks of these alternatives, share the discussion and conclusion with the broader campus community, and regularly evaluate if the policy continues to meet the institution's needs. Over time, the skills, investment performance, and ability to consistently add value change for money managers, so investment committees should thoroughly review all managers, including those who serve on the committee.

Investments Policy and Performance

To start the dialogue, investment committee members should ask:

- **Policy.** Are the investment policy and philosophy reviewed annually?
- **Adherence.** Is adherence to the investment policy reviewed at every committee meeting? Are deviations to the policy, including asset allocation directives and diversification, acknowledged?
- **Liquidity.** Is a liquidity policy in place that supports the institution's operating needs and potential call on capital for committed investments? Is it followed?
- **Information sharing.** Does the committee regularly report investment performance to the full board?

The investment committee is responsible for periodically reviewing and revising, as needed, the investment or endowment policy. Generally, an endowment policy has four goals:

1. Provide current institutional support;
2. Provide future institutional support;
3. Maintain sustainable payout levels; and
4. Ensure predictability of distributions.

Exhibit 13: **Commonfund's Risk Factors**

Strategic Risk—A forward-looking, top-down stress/scenario assessment of the potential impact to the organization's long-term strategy and investment policy due to fundamental shifts in external factors.

Investment Risk—Covers all aspects of market risk as well as the returns associated with any investment. This risk also assesses the potential gain distribution to ensure that any investment opportunity offers the potential for a consistent, risk adjusted return over time.

Operational Risk—Risk of loss resulting from human error or failed internal processes or systems, or from external events.

Balance Sheet Risk—Any risk that may affect the organization's balance sheet, such as short- to intermediate-term financing, swap transactions to manage interest rate exposure, swaps to manage currency exposure, and other structured products.

Credit/Counter-party Risk—Any risk associated with exposure to, or dealing with certain counter-parties. Typically includes an assessment of creditworthiness of one's trading counter-parties using market indicators such as long- and short-term credit ratings, spreads, trading indicators. Also includes any action to mitigate potential exposure to these counter-parties (for example, collateral management).

By-product Risk—Risk that arises through the interplay of all the risk types and the need for active risk mitigation.

Liquidity Risk—Decomposition of the investment portfolio by immediate cash requirements, liquid strategies, and illiquid strategies.

For more information, visit www.commonfund.org.

In evaluating its endowment policy, the investment committee should consider a variety of risks related to invested assets *(see Exhibit 13)*. Unfortunately, just when investment returns are expected to be more volatile and produce lower than historic averages, colleges, universities, and foundations are more reliant on returns to fill gaps left by declines in other sources of support. The more dependent an institution is on the endowment to support operations, the more risk the investment committee faces as it go about its work. Even institutions that have modest or no endowment face increased pressure to find investment yields on operating reserves that are safe and keep pace with inflation.

Development Committee

Ensuring the future of an institution also means planning and executing successful fundraising campaigns to support annual operations and long-term plans. A development committee and, in the case of some public universities, the foundation

---

Insight: Look carefully and closely at liquidity

In the current environment, liquidity risk deserves special attention. The inability to access funds for operational needs or to meet obligations of private equity investments became shockingly real after credit markets froze in 2008. Investment committees should establish a liquidity policy for investments that balances the advantages of longer term investments with the risk of not being able to meet capital calls and ongoing operational needs.

Sample Liquidity Policy

Asset	Liquidity	Policy
Liquid assets	At least quarterly	30% minimum
	Daily	10% minimum
Semi-liquid quarterly	< 3 years	35% maximum
Illiquid and unfunded commitments	> 3 years	40% maximum

Reprinted with permission from Whitman College.

---

board provide broad oversight of the institution's fundraising and friend-raising programs. The scope and corresponding risks that fall under the purview of the development committee include:

- Comprehensive campaigns;
- Gift policies;
- Board member philanthropy; and
- Support for advancement, fundraising, and marketing.

This is not a complete list; new risks will emerge over time, and some of these risks may not be relevant to every institution. But, for the vast majority of independent colleges and universities and related foundations, development committees should understand that these areas pose potential risk, and use that knowledge to ensure that potential gaps in risk identification are revealed and comprehensive mitigation plans are adhered to.

Some of the risks noted above are among the top concerns in higher education today. For example, the viability of a comprehensive campaign often heads the list of concerns among many institutions. Every higher education institution and foundation should have a fundraising or development plan that includes both annual and multiyear fundraising plans. The scope of the plans will determine the resources needed to be successful.

The development committee should understand the variety of risks related to fundraising, discuss them with administrators, and report their recommendations and conclusions to the full board.[31] The development committee should expect to see annual risk reports from the president or executive director and chief development officer designating the owner(s) of the top fundraising risks and progress toward mitigation plans.

Comprehensive Campaigns

To start the conversations, development committee members should ask:

- **Strategic alignment.** Is the case for launching a comprehensive campaign clear and aligned with the strategic plan of the institution?
- **Trustee commitment.** Are current and prospective trustees personally committed to contributing a substantial gift, their time, and their connections to the campaign?
- **Resources.** Does the institution have sufficient professional staff, training for volunteers, and infrastructure to support the multiyear effort?
- **Budget.** Is there a realistic budget and funds to support the annual operations of the campaign?
- **Integrity.** Are strong policies and procedures in place to ensure integrity in the acceptance, naming opportunities, and accounting for all gifts?
- **Gift policy.** Are policies and procedures in place to ensure that gifts are used for their intended purposes?
- **Progress reports.** Does the board receive regular reports on the progress of the campaign, including the net present value and face value of all gifts, including deferred gifts?

---

[31] For additional resources from AGB, see:
- Bass, David. "College Fundraising: Is There a 'New Normal'?" *Trusteeship*, November/December 2009.
- Helm, Peyton R. *The Development Committee* (Effective Committee Series), 2012.
- Legon, Richard D. *The Board's Role in Fundraising* (Board Basics), 2003.
- Worth, Michael J. *Securing the Future: A Fund-Raising Guide for Boards of Independent Colleges and Universities*, 2005.

Comprehensive campaigns are big business. They are complex and multi-year. They depend on an army of staff, volunteers, and consultants. They require specialized software, extensive travel, event planning, and sophisticated recordkeeping that can tax even the largest, most complex university. Board members perform a critical role in the planning and execution of comprehensive campaigns. They not only approve the strategic and fundraising plans, they are also the foundation—through their contributions and ability to open doors—of every successful comprehensive campaign.

Successful comprehensive campaigns align mission, strategic plans, and annual operating needs. Although the primary motivation for any campaign is to raise money to support strategic and operating plans, successful campaigns are also used to enhance the institution's reputation, raise visibility, boost morale, and elevate its mission and vision. They can also help identify and reconnect with alumni, local businesses, and even prospective students. But a campaign launched before an institution is ready can cause significant damage and turn those positives into negatives.[32]

Development committees should be alert to some of the most common campaign risks, which often stem from poor planning at the early stages, including the following five areas:

1. **Case statement:** Comprehensive campaigns begin with a strong case. The president often takes the lead on articulating the case and describing the vision for the future of the institution. The development committee then scrutinizes, discusses, and ultimately recommends its approval to the full board. At this initial stage, the greatest risk is a weak case. Failing to clearly articulate the rationale for asking donors to dig deep into personal resources to support the institution can doom a campaign.

2. **Campaign readiness:** After building a case—which should involve extensive discussions with a wide range of constituents—the development committee must assess the campaign readiness of the institution. Often,

---

[32] For additional resources from AGB, see Schrum, Jake B. (editor). *A Board's Guide to Comprehensive Campaigns*, 2000.

an outside consulting firm will conduct a campaign readiness or feasibility study. The results should not be ignored. A common risk is a desire by the administration or the board to proceed before addressing any challenges or weaknesses identified in the study.

3. **Development infrastructure:** Comprehensive campaigns are expensive and require steady resources to ensure success. Development committees are responsible for ensuring that the institution has allocated adequate resources to launch and sustain the campaign. Benchmarks are available to compare proposed budgets and assess the adequacy of resources. The most notable risk in this area is a lack of appreciation for the additional expenses related to a campaign and underinvestment in staffing and related expenses.

4. **Campaign costs:** Before starting the campaign, the development committee needs to decide how the institution will pay for the campaign costs. Will expenses come from unrestricted gifts, the institution's operating budget, as a tax or portion of every gift collected, or (if an institution is fortunate) from a donor through a designated gift? Careful attention should be paid to clearly disclose to all prospective donors whether a portion of a gift will be used to support campaign operations.

5. **Volunteer training:** Successful capital campaigns rely on a cadre of volunteers to solicit gifts. Training and support for these volunteers is critical to ensure the integrity of the message, appropriate follow-through, and ongoing positive relations with this important constituency. As volunteers themselves, development committee members are well positioned to evaluate the readiness and needs of other volunteers to support the campaign effort.

Once a comprehensive campaign is under way, many of the development committee's responsibilities parallel those of its ongoing oversight responsibilities (for example, gift-acceptance policies, compliance with donor intent, and ethical fundraising practices), described as follows.

Gift-Related Policies

The development committee, in collaboration with senior administrators, is responsible for ensuring that the college, university, or foundation has and follows appropriate policies and practices in terms of donor intent, internal gift acceptance and recordkeeping, and fundraising ethics.

Several high-profile lawsuits, which alleged that institutions did not follow donor intent on gift uses, put this issue in newspaper headlines and on board meeting agendas. Ensuring compliance with donor intent requires institution-wide coordination and communication. On the front end, the development committee and the administration should ensure that policies and procedures are in place for communicating donor intent. Then, the administration (through the development office) is responsible for 1) recording the donor's intent and the institution's agreement on the specific use of the gift, 2) communicating donor intent to the relevant departments, and 3) monitoring ongoing compliance with those intentions. Through the internal audit function or periodic review by external auditors, the administration and development committee can monitor adherence to gift use policies.

The development committee is also responsible for protecting the institution's tax-exempt status when it comes to fundraising and gift acceptance. It should ensure compliance with federal and state laws related to charitable contributions, as well as state fundraising registration requirements. Looking internally, the development committee should ensure that gift-acceptance policies have been established and are followed (especially for non-cash gifts, such as real estate and securities). It should ensure equal treatment in crediting gifts, and that institutional naming policies are followed. It should assure donor confidentiality when requested and allowed. *(Public institutions and related foundations may have unique challenges in assuring confidentiality, as discussed in the next section on foundations.)*

Last but not least, the development committee should pay attention to fundraising integrity. It should encourage and support a culture of ethical fundraising. It should ensure solicitation and acceptance of gifts that are appropriate for the mission of the institution. It should also seek ways to prevent development staff and the president from benefiting personally through commissions, personal gifts, or other benefits. For example, the institution should encourage donors to consult with their personal tax and legal advisors, and the institution's legal counsel should be involved in major (and planned) gift agreements and pledges.

Institutionally Related Foundations

Since the middle of the 20th century, institutionally related foundations have supported a "margin of excellence" at public colleges and universities by generating financial support that supplements tuition and state funding. They are tax-exempt, charitable organizations that may accept tax-deductible contributions to support the institution pursuant to Internal Revenue Code sections 170(b)(1)(A)(iv) and 501(c)(3). Over the years, the mission of related foundations has expanded to include certain duties that the public universities cannot perform under state law, such as accepting charitable contributions. In practice, foundations enable public universities to access private funds for research, scholarships, and other activities areas.[33]

Varying widely from institution to institution, foundation responsibilities may include, but are not limited to, management of the endowment, real estate, and intellectual property; donor and alumni record-keeping; and purchasing—all pursued in support of the mission and goals of the respective public college or university. In today's increasingly competitive world, foundations allow public institutions to better compete with independent colleges and universities that have endowments. Experts in higher education anticipate that foundations supporting public institutions—from community colleges to comprehensive research universities—will gain in importance as public support of higher education continues to decline.

This section addresses issues *unique* to foundations that support public institutions; other sections in the book address risks that are common to most boards

---

[33] For additional resources from AGB, see
- Legon, Richard D. (editor) *Margin of Excellence: The New Work of Higher Education Foundations*, 2005.
- Worth, Michael J. *Foundations for the Future: The Fundraising Role of Foundation Boards at Public Colleges and Universities*, 2012.
- Bass, David and Jim Lanier, "What Lies Ahead for University-Foundation Relations?" *Trusteeship*, November/December 2008.
- Bass, David. "What's a Prudent Payout from an 'Underwater' Endowment?" *Trusteeship*, May/June 2009.

and managed through committees (such as investment, governance, and development). Risks specific to foundation boards include:

- State laws and regulations, including freedom of information;
- Board membership and conflicts of interest; and
- Administrative support and shared services.

To start the dialogue, foundation board members should ask:

- **Delineation of roles.** Are the functions of the foundation and institution clearly delineated and understood by board members and staff of both?
- **Separation of operations.** Are policies and procedures separating the operations of the foundation and institution developed with guidance of legal counsel? Are they strictly adhered to?
- **Open-records laws.** Does the foundation comply with state requirements for open records? Where possible, does it protect the confidentiality of donors?

Foundation-Institution Relations

Establishing clear distinctions on the roles and responsibilities of the foundation staff and board members and adherence to a memorandum of understanding between the university and the foundation are best practices. Although state laws vary greatly, most foundations will not be able to accept any state funding, if they want to operate independently. A new foundation will be particularly challenged as it begins operations, reimbursing the university for any services it provides to the foundation and maintaining financial independence without endowment support.

The greatest risk for a foundation is the reputational risk to the institution it supports that comes with a breach of public trust. Adherence by the university to gift-use policies and following the donor's intent of the gift is critical for the foundation board to monitor.

Open-Records Laws

The scrutiny of foundation policies and practices from the press and public has increased in recent years. High-profile cases of alleged misuse of funds and court rulings imposing state open-records standards on related foundations raise the risks that a foundation will not be able to achieve its mission in support of the institution including maintaining anonymity for donors that request it.

Foundations that rely on the college or university for resources such as information technology (including data storage), office space and facilities, human resources (for example, shared staff), and accounting functions should understand the structure of their relationship, the autonomy of the foundation, and relevant state laws. Because this is a complex and evolving area, the foundation board should use legal counsel and association resources to stay abreast of changes in state regulations and court rulings that may necessitate changes in how the institution and foundation operate in support of their respective missions.

Foundations and Open-Records Laws

The Student Press Law Center lists the following factors as influential in successfully litigating the applicability of a state's open-records laws to a related foundation:

1. Whether the foundation shares the same directors with the university;
2. Whether it uses university employees;
3. Whether it uses university property or resources;
4. Whether it receives state funds; and
5. Whether it is responsible for managing university assets.

The center notes in its tip sheet, "Unfortunately, courts ranked the relative importance of each factor differently and one judge's analysis may not prevail in a neighboring jurisdiction."

Source: "Tip Sheet: Access to University Foundation Records." Student Press Law Center, 2010. For more information, see www.splc.org.

7

OPERATIONAL RISKS

Board committees that oversee the operations of the institution and the corresponding risks, set college and universities apart from corporate boards. While corporate boards are normally limited to audit, governance, compensation, and executive committees, higher education institutions traditionally maintain board committees with oversight for the core operations of the institution: academic affairs, student/campus life, and facilities. These operating committees provide guidance and support for the mission of the institution—teaching, research, and service. It is not the role of the committees to manage these functions but it is their responsibility to understand, question, and ultimately support the direction set by the strategic plan and implemented through the annual operations. Committee oversight requires strong knowledge of potential risks.

Academic Affairs Committee

The academic affairs committee is one of the busiest intersections of shared governance. On behalf of the governing board, the academic affairs committee bears the primary responsibility for defining, overseeing, and modifying the policies that fulfill a college or university's academic mission. This includes what students learn and how well they learn it; the effectiveness of teaching and learning; faculty selection, recognition, and development; how to assess and reward teaching excellence; efficient and sensible organization of departments, divisions, and colleges within larger institutions; academic standards and requirements; and the appropriate balance among teaching, scholarship, and service—among many other elements. The risks that come under the purview of academic affairs include:

- Academic quality;
- Accreditation;
- Blended (online) learning;
- Faculty conflicts of interest;
- Faculty recruitment;
- International programs and global strategy;
- Medical centers;
- Program closures;
- New programs and entrepreneurial ventures;
- Research;
- Outcomes; and
- Tenure and promotion.

This is not a complete list; new risks will inevitably emerge, and some risks may not be relevant to all colleges, universities, and systems. The academic affairs committee is tasked with understanding the areas that pose the greatest risk to the institution, helping to identify potential gaps in risk identification and ensuring that mitigation plans are developed and followed. The committee should work closely with senior members of the administration and receive annual reports that designate the owner of the risk and document progress on mitigation plans. (*See page 19, Exhibit 7, for a sample report, and page 132, Appendix A, for a sample academic affairs risk register.*)

The following discussions focus on some of the most common, challenging, and significant risks related to academic affairs, including:

- Academic quality;
- Tenure;
- Starting and closing programs;
- Research;
- International programs; and
- Medical centers.

The following pages are intended to offer insights to members of the board and the academic affairs committee so that they are better prepared to explore the risks and contribute to productive conversations with administrators. The academic affairs committee should expect to see annual risk reports from senior administrators that designate the owner(s) of the top risks and document progress toward mitigation plans.

Academic Quality

To start the dialogue, the academic affairs committee should ask administrators:

1. How good is our product?
2. How good are we at producing our product?
3. Are our customers satisfied?
4. Do we have the right mix of products?
5. Do we "make the grade"?

The spotlight on academic quality is growing brighter as students, parents, legislators, and employers question the effectiveness of courses taught at colleges and universities and the skills graduates bring to the workplace. According to a 2011 Gallup/Lumina Education Foundation survey, 86 percent of the American public believe the main reason to pursue education past high school is to get a better job and/or earn more money. Only 5 percent believe the purpose is to become a more well-rounded adult, and 1 percent believe the purpose is to learn to think more critically. The concept of a traditional undergraduate education is evolving, which brings increased scrutiny and new risks to leaders in higher education. In short, students and families are questioning the value of an education and the return on their investment.

While many board members are used to measuring financial health, tracking financial ratios, and reviewing balance sheets, overseeing the quality of the academic experience is new territory for most board members. The board needs to ask the administration if the perceived quality of the academic "product" and experience at the institution is sufficient to give the institution tuition pricing power. In light of the public's perception of the value of a college degree, can an institution market and sustain its traditional curriculum? If the institution is unable to align the academic program with student demand, and enrollment slips and tuition discounts increase, the institution may be on an unsustainable path. Instructional strategy is the responsibility of the faculty; ensuring that appropriate financial resources support that strategy is the responsibility of the president and board.[34]

The role of the board in academic quality can be a sensitive topic. The concept of shared governance keeps boards from developing or modifying curriculum, which is generally accepted as the sole province of the faculty. In ensuring academic quality—and mitigating risks that arise when the quality of the educational experience is less than students and parents can reasonably expect—the board's role is to remind faculty of their responsibility for developing curriculum and hold them accountable for its continuous improvement. In doing this, boards must walk a fine line.

> "Some colleges will choose to embrace a mission and accept the consequences to their revenue. Others will choose to pursue revenue and accept the consequences to their mission."
>
> —Nathan Mueller, principal, Hardwick-Day

Disruptive innovations in teaching and learning have further complicated oversight of educational quality. In the past, instructional strategy meant a faculty member deciding if a course would be better taught as a seminar or lecture. Now, instructional strategy might encompass not only lectures, seminars, labs, internships, externships, and service learning but also campus-based or distance e-learning, massive open online courses (MOOCs), social media, and the like. And, there are risks at both ends of the blended learning continuum. Some universities (sometimes driven by the board) are rushing to participate in MOOCs without a full evaluation of how they fit within the institution's instructional strategy, broader strategic plans, brand, and overall financial picture. Other (often small, independent) colleges are choosing to ignore or downplay digital learning opportunities, assuming that this trend will pass. All institutions must recognize that blended learning instruction must also meet accessibility standards of the Americans with Disabilities Act.

---

[34] For additional resources from AGB, see:
- Ewell, Peter. *Making the Grade: How Boards Can Ensure Academic Quality*, 2nd Edition, 2012.
- Green, Kenneth C. "Mission, MOOCs, and Money." *Trusteeship*, January/February 2013.
- "How Boards Oversee Educational Quality: A Report on a Survey of the Assessment of Student Learning." 2010.
- *Statement on Board Responsibility for the Oversight of Educational Quality*, 2010.
- Twigg, Carol A. "Transforming Learning Through Technology: Educating More, Costing Less." *Trusteeship*, September/October 2011.
- Wood, Richard. *The Academic Affairs Committee* (Effective Committee Series), 1997.

Discussions within the academic affairs committee and with faculty leadership are a good starting place to ensure that instructional strategy and resource requirements are aligned. The academic affairs committee can help the board oversee educational quality by embracing the following five principles:

1. Curriculum is the faculty's responsibility; the board's role is to remind them of that responsibility.
2. Stay focused on strategic issues.
3. Expect and demand a culture of evidence.

Oversight of Educational Quality: If not the board, then who?

"There are reasons, of course, for keeping boards out of educational issues. Most college trustees are business executives or lawyers with no special knowledge of academic matters. Moreover education, like art and architecture, is a subject on which many inexperienced observers feel entitled to express views, views strongly held but often quite wrong. To faculty members, then, and even presidents, the prospect of having a board look at any part of the educational process may well seem threatening.

"Yet self-restraint also has its costs. Who else is capable of altering the current system of incentives and rewards to hold deans and presidents accountable for the quality of their educational leadership? No faculty ever forced its leaders out for failing to act vigorously enough to improve the prevailing methods of education. On the contrary, faculties are more likely to resist any determined effort to examine their work and question familiar ways of teaching and learning. Students cannot tell whether current practices are less effective than they might be. Alumni are too far removed to know what needs to be done. As a result, if trustees ignore the subject, there may be no one to press academic leaders to attend to those aspects of the education program that are in greatest need of reform.

"Fortunately, the risks of unwise intervention are fairly low, so long as trustees do not try to dictate what courses should be taught and what instructional methods employed but merely ask for reports on the procedures used to evaluate academic programs and encourage innovation. It is surely within the prerogatives of the board to take an interest in these activities and to urge the president to work with the faculty to develop a process designed to ensure continuing improvement in the quality of education...

"Although...trustees can provide an important impetus for reform, and back it stoutly when it occurs, they cannot guarantee change by their own efforts. They can urge a process of self-scrutiny and innovation and give it greater legitimacy, but they cannot bring it about themselves. Real improvement requires the initiative and skills of academic leaders—presidents, provosts, and deans—who understand what needs to be done and appeal successfully to the sense of professional responsibility that most faculties share for the education of their students."

—Derek C. Bok, former president, Harvard University

Source: Derek Bok. *Our Underachieving Colleges: A Candid Look at How Much Students Learn and Why They Should be Learning More.* New Jersey: Princeton University Press, 2006. pp. 333-335.

4. Recognize that evidence about academic quality raises issues but rarely gives final answers.

5. Make reviewing evidence of academic quality and improvement a regular and expected board-level activity.

Tenure

To start the dialogue, the academic affairs committee can ask administrators the following questions (given their import, these questions are normally discussed with the full board, not exclusively within the academic affairs committee):

- **Legal review.** Have the faculty handbook and tenure policies been reviewed recently by legal counsel with expertise in higher education employment law?

- **Adherence to policies.** Are tenure review committees trained to ensure current practices adhere to the institution's policies and faculty handbook?

- **Best practices.** Has the institution incorporated the advice for institutional best practices in tenure evaluation as promulgated by the American Council on Education (ACE), American Association of University Professors (AAUP), and United Educators (UE)?

- **Litigation.** If tenure litigation becomes inevitable, does the board have a process for testing its resolve?

Tenure as an employment agreement is unlike what board members experience in business, government, or nonprofit organizations. The tenure process and the academic freedom it protects bring unique risks to higher education. In 1994, Congress allowed a special exemption to the Age Discrimination in Employment Act to expire, prohibiting colleges and universities from enforcing mandatory retirement at age 70.

The findings from jury research, conducted by United Educators in 2011, offer a lesson for academic affairs committee and board members. In "Lessons from Costly Tenure Denial Claims," D. Frank Vinik reported that the American public does not understand academic tenure and 70 percent of respondents would find a faculty member more believable than a university. So, it behooves the administration to educate the

---

Exhibit 14: **Best Practices in Tenure Evaluation—the Four C's**

- **Clarity** in standards and procedures for tenure evaluation
  - Tenure policy should comprehensively list all major criteria used for evaluation and all tenure evaluators should know—and apply—the criteria.

- **Consistency** in tenure decisions
  - Faculty, administration and board should ensure long-term consistency in the review of all faculty, and career counseling for non-tenured faculty should be consistent with tenure requirements.

- **Candor** in the evaluation of tenure-track faculty
  - Faculty leaders and administrators should provide all tenure-track faculty with a clear explanation of requirements for tenure and clear advice at regular intervals about progress in meeting requirements.

- **Caring** for unsuccessful candidates
  - A negative tenure decision should be delivered with compassion, and institutional support should be provided to help the unsuccessful candidate get back on his/her feet elsewhere.

Source: "Good Practice in Tenure Evaluation: Advice for Tenured Faculty, Department Chairs, and Academic Administrators." American Council on Education, American Association of University Professors, and United Educators, 2000.

---

board—as a university would educate a jury—about the meaning of tenure and the relative weight of research and teaching as promotion criteria.[35]

According to a 2011 United Educators claims study, while faculty brought only 30 percent of the employment claims received over a five-year period, the cost of faculty employment lawsuits was 43 percent of the total amount spent. A substantial number of the claims and costs were for tenure denial and tenure revocation. While there is an ongoing debate on the future of tenure, leaders at institutions with tenured faculty face increased risks in lawsuits if the tenure processes and policies are not clear, fair, and consistently followed. *(See Exhibit 14.)*

Tenure litigation is one of the most expensive, divisive, and time-consuming risks that educational institutions face. The stakes are extremely high. The core of a tenure denial or tenure revocation lawsuit focuses on lifetime employment and all of the security and prestige associated with the position. Although much rarer than the denial of tenure for assistant professors, tenure revocation does occur and often

---

[35] For additional resources from AGB, see:
- Trower, Cathy A. "Academic Tenure and the Traditional Assumptions Boards Should Question." *Trusteeship*, November/December 2012.
- Bernard, Pamela J., Thomas A. Gottschalk, and Robert M. O'Neil. "Why Boards Can't Ignore Academic Freedom." *Trusteeship*, July/August 2011.

leads to litigation. Should a lawsuit seem imminent, the board and administration, together, need to ask and answer the following questions:

1. Is there a critical principle at stake?
2. Is the institution willing to withstand negative publicity?
3. How much will the case cost to take to trial?
4. Are the president and academic leadership willing to devote time for the trial, including depositions, testifying, and attending the trial?
5. What are the chances of prevailing at trial?

Litigation management is not the direct responsibility of the board, but board members play a role in supporting the president and academic leadership as the case develops. Tenure litigation cases often involve whole departments, often on opposing sides of the tenure denial; students, who may appreciate the professor's teaching style but not understand the institution's research agenda; and alumni. Adding to the turmoil surrounding tenure disputes is the information that becomes public during litigation. This may include the tenure files of the faculty member bringing the suit, with all of the accompanying recommendations, outside evaluations, committee notes, and frequently the tenure files of other faculty in the institution (the "comparators" used to evaluate the institution's process, consistency, and fairness). Notes that were written years ago, and presumed to be confidential, can become part of a public trial. The bitterness and divisiveness that tenure litigation provokes can last for years and in some cases decades.

Insight: Beware faint praise

During "Good Practice in Tenure Evaluation" workshops for faculty tenure committees, the most engaged discussions are on case studies about candor and consistency. The workshops reveal that senior faculty have a tendency to offer faint praise in interim evaluations. Then, when denied tenure, candidates are surprised and angry. They need legal hooks to sue, which are usually discrimination and breach of contract.

Frequently some evidence shows that the candidate was treated differently, which goes to consistency. Often, however, the most damning evidence is that the process was not fair and senior faculty had a cavalier attitude toward mentoring the candidate and offering constructive feedback to improve performance. This can be a powerful argument that juries easily understand. Lawsuits are often settled, not because discrimination actually occurred, but because of a concern that a jury would sympathize with the candidate and find a way to compensate him or her for shoddy treatment in a career-determining process.

Program Changes: Starting New Programs and Closing Programs

The academic affairs committee need not review business plans for each new program or entrepreneurial venture. Rather, it should make sure that the administration has rigorous planning, management, and monitoring policies and procedures and that they are followed. To start the dialogue, the academic affairs committee should ask administrators:

- **New program planning.** Is there a detailed business plan to support each new program?
- **Annual reviews.** Are there annual reviews of ongoing programs to test the validity of assumptions, progress toward accreditation, financial results, and strength and relationship of all partners?
- **Program closure.** When considering closing programs, are the key constituents involved? Are considerations related to faculty and students taken into account?

A significant shift occurring at colleges and universities is the pressure to become more entrepreneurial. These entrepreneurial initiatives may be domestic or international, online and through branch campuses, initiated alone or with partners. Their pace and scope are increasing. New programs are pursued for a variety of reasons: to strengthen the core mission of the institution, to meet new and evolving constituent needs, and often to add revenue to replace declining state and family support.

For purposes of this discussion, programs are broadly defined to be an academic program, department, or school within a larger institution. Especially for new programs, the rush to market poses heightened financial and reputational risks. Some of the most common problems relate to outsourcing, accreditation, and academic quality. The academic affairs committee, in conjunction with other committees, should make sure that business planning exercises include the following:

- External market research validating demand for the new program;
- Pro forma financial plan with clear explanations of assumptions;
- Legal review of contracts, including employment, facilities, operations, and others;

- Documentation of accreditation required for successful program operation, with special attention to requirements needed to sit for external exams and licenses;
- Review of consumer protection statutes and their applicability to proposed courses and programs of study;
- Thorough review of marketing materials to ensure compliance with consumer protection laws, providing appropriate disclaimers for accreditation and potential future employment of program graduates; and
- Training for program administrators, including admissions staff, to ensure understanding of consumer protection laws.

As campuses evaluate new programs, ongoing reviews of current programs can result in a recommendation by the faculty and administration to close a program that no longer supports the mission, has shrinking enrollments, or can be better served through collaboration with another institution. Program closures can lead to lengthy and expensive lawsuits and reputational damage if not managed appropriately. Potential lawsuits can come from faculty and staff who may be terminated, students who may allege a breach of contract or consumer fraud, or partners who may allege a breach of contract. Boards should recognize that closing a program is

Case in Point: Tales of caution from the claims files

Accreditation status hits a snag: A comprehensive university contracted with an outside partner to run a program for medical assistants. The program was run under the university's name but operated by the outside firm. Students were told that the program was fully accredited and that they would be able to sit for the three required licensing exams. However, the accreditation was only secured for two exams. Former students alleged that they were misled about the accreditation status. When the university applied to extend the accreditation to the third exam, it was denied. Then the outside partner experienced financial difficulties, leaving the university to settle the lawsuits.

Quality control gets squeezed: A university offered financial incentives to departments and individual professors to teach short-term, offsite courses in several information technology disciplines. Recruiters promised Microsoft certification upon completion. In the rush to market, departmental oversight was not up to the same level demanded on the main campus. Course materials were late arriving at the offsite locations and, in some cases, not current. The coursework did not lead students to the desired certifications. The university refunded tuition. But, a group of students sued the institution, alleging it violated the state's deceptive trade practices act by luring them to quit steady jobs to take this certification course.

not inexpensive, but, done well, the reputational damage will be minimized and the campus can focus on its ongoing mission.

When confronting a program closure, the academic affairs committee should ask administrators the following questions:

- **Closure planning.** Were faculty involved in the review and decision to close a program? Were alternatives to closing the program considered?
- **Personnel matters.** Is outside legal counsel with experience in reductions in force involved if faculty or employee layoffs are contemplated? Does the faculty handbook offer a definition and guidance for financial exigency if faculty positions are terminated? Are provisions established to help and support both terminated and remaining employees?
- **Student concerns.** Does the student handbook state that the institution reserves the right to terminate and reduce programs when deemed necessary by the institution? Is there a plan in place to "teach out" enrolled students or assist in transfers to other institutions?

International Programs

To start the dialogue, the academic affairs committee can ask administrators about:

- **Due diligence.** Has appropriate due diligence been completed on all partners, suppliers, and agents involved in international programs?
- **Compliance.** Has a compliance checklist covering domestic and foreign regulations been developed and reviewed by counsel with expertise in international business and local counsel in the country of the foreign program?
- **Intellectual property.** Has the institution's name and intellectual property been registered and protected in foreign countries in which it will be doing business?
- **Exit strategy.** Does the institution have an exit strategy if the international program is terminated? Do agreements have clear guidance on dispute resolution?
- **Sponsored research.** Are the proper controls in place to ensure that sponsored research in the U.S., involving non-U.S. citizens, students, and

faculty complies with security and other government regulations?

- **Foreign recruiters.** If independent foreign agencies are used to recruit international students, are the agencies appropriately trained on the institution's standards, are the contracts regularly reviewed, and does the board support the compensation terms?
- **Contingency plans.** Are there contingency plans to accommodate a sudden and unexpected drop in international students and faculty, as happened after the 2001 terrorist attacks?

While many colleges and universities are building a global curriculum and experience for their students and faculty in myriad ways, the most common international strategies and their attendant academic-related risks often fall into one of three areas: overseas campuses, international recruiting, and study abroad programs *(See Student Affairs Committee, Study Abroad Programs, page 119)*.

Increasingly, large colleges and universities are building branch or independent campuses overseas, sometimes on their own and sometimes in partnership with a local entity. The complexity of these ventures requires working with legal and academic experts who understand U.S. law and that of host countries. Initial areas to address in starting a formal program in another country include protecting the institution's name and intellectual property, adhering to U.S. laws safeguarding financial transactions, and establishing a clear understanding of faculty and administrator employment status. Before embarking on a new initiative, the academic affairs committee (in conjunction with other committees) should ensure that there is regular reporting on the academic programs and financial status, as well as a carefully designed exit strategy should the findings suggest the need to end the program.

Recruiting international students and faculty to study and teach at U.S. campuses is also on the rise. For many colleges and universities, international

Case in Point: Know how to fold 'em

A university operated a campus in Europe, first working with the U.S. military and then through a nonprofit organization. After an external audit revealed ongoing financial problems, the program closed. A number of lawsuits from students, faculty, and the former campus president followed the campus closing. Allegations included the violation of employment contracts, and the faculty was confused as to who owned the campus and which employment laws (European Union or U.S.) were applicable. Students were concerned about recovering paid tuition. The lawsuits from the former president, staff, and students continued for many years.

students are an increasingly important part of admissions strategies. A research report from World Education Services (WES), a credential evaluation organization, identifies several risk factors related to international students. While they use institutional websites, education fairs, social media sites, and agents to learn about U.S. colleges and universities, international students with low-level academic preparedness are more likely to use agents to find a U.S. college or university.

Institutions that depend on agents to attract international students must, according to WES, "realistically assess their capacity to provide ample academic support—such as English-as-a-second-language (ESL) and foundation courses— to international students." In addition, the use of agents is controversial at many campuses. Federal law prohibits compensating recruiters on a per-student basis for domestic students, and many believe these same standards should apply to recruiting international students. The academic affairs committee, in conjunction with the student affairs committee, should understand the recruiting practices in place for international students and discuss the institution's preparedness to accommodate the students and integrate them into academic programs.[36] *(See also Student Affairs Committee, Admissions, Enrollment, and Retention, page 104.)*

Research

To start the dialogue, the academic affairs committee should ask administrators:

- **Need.** Does the research agenda support the college or university's mission and priorities? Will the research fill an unmet need?
- **Total cost.** What is the total cost of new research initiatives, including the cost of constructing and maintaining facilities and infrastructure, supporting faculty and graduate students, and maintaining program operations?
- **Funding.** Does the university acknowledge the potential instability of outside support for research? Has senior leadership articulated the amount of internal funding that will be needed to support the research programs?

---

[36] For additional resources from AGB, see:
- Lovett, Clara M. "Going Global: Dispatches from Experienced Board Members." *Trusteeship*, November/December 2011.
- Bernard, Pamela J. "Presidents and Boards Must Be Deliberate as They Expand International Activities." *Trusteeship*, July/August 2008.

- **Compliance.** What funding exists for administrative oversight to ensure compliance with federal, state, and corporate mandates?
- **Conflicts of interest.** Does the university follow conflict of interest policies governing researchers' connections to funding sources and potential business ventures?
- **Technology transfer.** Do intellectual property policies clarify the roles of faculty researchers and the university to support technology transfer?
- **Reputation risks.** What are the potential reputational risks to the university for research misconduct?
- **Crisis planning.** Are there protocols in place to secure research (for example, materials in storage, animals, data) in the event of power outage, natural disaster or human error? Is there a recovery plan in place in the event of a crisis?

Basic research in the United States has been a partnership between federal and state governments and universities since the passing of the Morrill Act in 1862. What began as a focus on the challenges to a young country as it addressed an agricultural and emerging industrial economy has evolved into a driving force in innovation and technological improvements, from DNA fingerprinting to weather forecasting to the global positioning system and beyond. Boards, administrators, and faculty at research universities wonder how this centuries-old partnership may change and what risks and opportunities await. In 2012, the National Academies' National Research Council (NRC) identified the following challenges:

- Federal funding for research universities has been unstable and, in real terms, is declining at a time when research and development in other countries (notably China and India) is increasing.
- State funding for higher education has been declining for several decades.
- Corporations have dismantled their research labs (for example, Bell Labs) yet have not developed partnerships for basic research with universities.
- Research at universities needs to improve management, productivity, and cost efficiency to be more effective and a better steward of scarce resources.

According to a 2012 National Science Foundation report, of the $55 billion in annual university research funding, approximately 60 percent comes from the federal government, 20 percent from universities' budgets, and 20 percent from corporations, states, and foundations. Furthermore, as NRC pointed out, this funding is precarious. In the last 10 years, federal support for university research declined from 70 percent to 60 percent, and universities themselves have increased their share of research funding. Major foundation support has grown modestly, and corporate support has declined slightly. Researchers seeking to offset declines in federal support with corporate funding must reconcile the corporations' requirements for guarding proprietary intellectual property with the university's interest in peer review, transparency, and sharing of academic knowledge.[37] *(See Exhibit 11, page 56.)*

Still, the federal government funds well over half of all university research. The cost of complying with federal and state regulations has increased dramatically, further burdening researchers and university administrators. Compliance and oversight covers a wide range of research activities, including animal and human subject protocols, export controls, intellectual property rights, scientific integrity, security, and safety. For example, research conducted in areas sensitive to national security carries added requirements, such as restrictions on access to labs and limitations on foreign student participation. Universities have noted an increased vigilance on the part of government agencies and inspectors general to investigate and prosecute institutions for non-compliance. Moreover, while expenses related to compliance and oversight have increased, limits have been placed on indirect cost recovery (the amount of administrative costs that can be recovered) from federal grants. Unfunded mandates for compliance are now an integral part of any basic research program.

At universities, the total cost of research is neither well understood nor completely accounted for, which threatens an institution's ability to sustain facilities and research staff. Campuses have traditionally taken the upfront risk building labs and investing in infrastructure with the hope that the cost of these capital invest-

---

[37] For additional information from AGB, see *Statement on External Influences on Universities and Colleges*, 2012.

ments will be covered in the future by indirect costs. That assumption is riskier now than it has ever been, and it warrants consideration by the academic affairs committee, as well as the finance committee.

As part of its risk management assessment, the academic affairs committee should also consider the processes and policies related to research. It should verify that policies and processes are in place to ensure the integrity of research findings and that honest and verifiable methods are used, that reports to funding agencies are timely and accurate, and that research practices reflect the institution's academic standards and professional norms. Appropriate training on the institution's standards—including ownership of intellectual property, publishing guidelines, effort reporting, and lab safety—should be in place and delivered to faculty, researchers, and students.

Academic research is an integral part of many universities but is often left out of business continuity plans. Valuable research materials and data have been lost when natural catastrophes hit campus buildings. Institutions struggle to find insurance coverage for many academic research projects, increasing the importance of including research labs in disaster preparedness drills and providing protection of research animals, tissue, and data with generators and environmental controls.

Federal Funding, Fraud, and Whistleblowers

Investigations under the federal False Claims Act (FCA) are a growing risk for institutions that receive federal support. The act imposes liability on individuals and institutions that defraud government programs. Although the FCA applies to misuse of any federal funds, research programs and misuse of Medicare funds generate the most lawsuits. The FCA includes rewards (known as a "qui tam" provision) and protection for whistleblowers who report misconduct on federal grants. Many states and some cities also maintain FCA regulations.

Retaliation claims by whistleblowers are among the costliest and most disruptive lawsuits for universities and can damage an institution's reputation. In these types of suits, a whistleblower typically alleges that he or she suffered reprisal for reporting or complaining about wrongdoing, such as misuse of federal funds or violations of overtime laws. Most colleges and universities already recognize the need to prevent retaliation following an employee complaint about discrimination or harassment on the basis of race, sex, or another protected category. But, they may not realize that they must be equally vigilant about preventing retaliation against employees who complain or simply raise questions about other types of illegal or improper conduct. Appropriate internal controls and audit functions, sound personnel practices (for example, grievance procedures and whistleblower policies), and training of supervisors can reduce the likelihood of FCA and retaliation claims.

Academic Medical Centers

Academic medical centers (AMCs) are often the most complex and challenging part of any university. Addressing the risks associated with these centers is a monumental task. On behalf of the governing board, the academic affairs committee can start the dialogue by asking administrators:

- **Strategy.** Does the AMC have a strategy in place to control costs and increase quality? Are merger and acquisition opportunities explored?
- **Innovation.** Does the AMC investigate innovative ways to attract and engage patients using new technology and delivery systems?
- **Data analytics.** Does the AMC harness data and analytics to improve delivery and patient care?
- **Mission alignment.** Are the research, clinical, and business strategies aligned to support the AMC's mission and focus on being a center of excellence?

AMCs support research, teaching, and clinical care and are the backbone of the American medical system. They train future health care providers, produce basic research and medical breakthroughs, and care for the most challenging and risky patients. AMCs are decentralized, and function with very slim operating financial margins. Significant changes brought on by the 2010 Affordable Care Act, such as increased demand for technology investments, pressure from consumers and health insurance providers to reduce costs and improve productivity, and shrinking federal support for basic research will create additional risks and opportunities for AMCs *(see Exhibit 15)*.

At the governing board level, and often through the academic affairs committee, issues that warrant careful consideration—above and beyond those particular to health care delivery—relate to financial and reputational assets. Some AMCs have separate, independent governing boards; others share board members or report to the university's governing board. The separation of reporting and fiduciary responsibilities, while important, does not address public perception of the link between the AMC and the university:[38]

---

[38] For additional resources from AGB, see Kirch, Darrell G. "Higher Education and Health Care at a Crossroads." *Trusteeship*, March/April 2011.

Exhibit 15: **3 Major Forces Requiring Academic Medical Centers to Change**

Force #1   *Reform rebound:* Budgetary and political issues will raise the threat level at AMCs. As national and state governments face budgetary pressures, AMCs will be compelled to play a part in finding savings and quality in both traditional and new government programs.

Force #2   *Brand breakdown:* Low quality rankings and imprudent affiliations could damage the AMC brand. The AMC brands are among the most powerful in health care, yet they do not score at the top of recent quality rankings, and the brand could be further diluted through poorly managed affiliations and partnerships with other hospitals.

Force #3   *Organizational misalignment:* Old AMC structure is not designed to address new challenges. The highly decentralized governance structures at AMCs threaten their ability to respond to the challenges of the current and future health care environment.

Source: PwC Health Research Institute Report. "The Future of Academic Medical Centers: Strategies to Avoid a Margin Meltdown," PricewaterhouseCoopers, 2012.

- The public will not differentiate an insurance fraud scandal at the university hospital from the university.

- Experts believe shrinking federal and state support for both reimbursement of services and basic research will lead to a further decline in net revenue for AMCs, which may strain the institution's financial health.

- The complexities of funding and cross-subsidization of clinical care, physician training, and research present unique challenges for governing boards and administrators. Clinical trials, vital to academic research, present a major risk in terms of overall patient safety and for potential conflicts of interest related to the funding source (such as for drug research), which may be linked to commercial interests.

Student Affairs Committee

College and university boards are charged with governance responsibility to ensure that students receive a high-quality education from a well-managed institution. Although many of the areas involving students and campus life cross over to other board committees (for example, study abroad programs may be addressed by the academic affairs committee, financial aid is increasingly a finance committee focus), the student affairs committee is charged with:

1. Ensuring that the best interests of students are at the center of board considerations and decisions;

2. Educating itself and the board about students attending the institution and the services in place to support them;

3. Promoting and supporting institutional efforts to create a climate that is focused on student engagement both inside and outside the classroom; and

4. Helping ensure that adequate resources for programs and services exist to support students in their learning and development.[39]

Risks that fall under the purview of the student affairs (sometimes called the campus life) committee may include:

- Admissions, enrollment, and student retention;
- Alcohol and drug use/policies;
- Athletics;
- Campus security and crime reporting;
- Care teams/threat assessment;
- Commuting student programs;
- Enrollment;
- Experiential learning;
- Family Educational Rights and Privacy Act (FERPA) compliance;
- Financial aid/student debt;
- Health and safety;
- International students;
- Minors on campus;
- Residence halls;
- Service learning programs;
- Sexual assault/Title IX compliance;
- Student health and mental health centers; and
- Study abroad.

---

[39] For additional resources from AGB, see Ellis, Shannon. *The Student Affairs Committee* (Effective Committee Series), 2012.

This is not a complete list; new risks will inevitably emerge, and some risks may not be relevant to all colleges, universities, and systems. The student affairs committee is tasked with understanding the areas that pose greatest risk to the institution, helping to identify potential gaps in risk identification, and ensuring that mitigation plans are developed and followed. The committee should work closely with senior members of the administration and receive annual reports that designate the owner of the risk and document progress on mitigation plans. *(See Appendix A, page 136, for sample risk register.)*

The following discussions focus on some of the most common, challenging, and significant risks related to academic quality. Unfortunately, some risks are, or have become, particularly high-profile issues for colleges and universities, including:

- Admissions, enrollments, and student retention;
- Health and safety, including alcohol and drug use, student health centers, student sexual assault, and minors on campus;
- Campus security, including crime reporting, guns, and emergency care teams;
- Athletics; and
- Student activities, including study abroad programs and clubs.

The following pages are intended to offer insights to members of the board and the academic affairs committee so that they are better prepared to explore the risks and contribute to productive conversations with administrators.

Admissions, Enrollments, and Student Retention

To start the dialogue, the student affairs committee can ask administrators:

- **Demographic shifts.** Does the institution have a plan in place to address potential shifts in demographics?
- **Analytics.** Are there reports and analysis that track the efficiency and effectiveness of admissions and retention strategies?

The admissions process has changed dramatically since the time most board members applied to college. The common application, multiple applications, social media, portals, and negotiating for financial aid are now fixtures on the admissions landscape. From an institution-wide perspective, however, the broader risks for admissions are whether the institution can attract, enroll, retain, and graduate students who will benefit from its particular academic and extracurricular programs.

Regional differences in high school graduation rates, college readiness, and college enrollment in the future will force many admissions officers to look beyond their traditional markets to identify the next generation of students. To help the institution move beyond its current student profile, the student affairs committee should encourage long-term analysis of admissions trends and creative approaches to recruitment.

Student retention and graduation rates are receiving increased attention hand-in-hand with increased student debt. Institutions expend tremendous effort and expense to attract students but often significantly less to retain them through graduation. The student affairs committee should review reports of retention rates and analyze the reasons students do not persist to degree completion.

The high-pressure sales tactics used by some for-profit institutions, which have caught the eye of the federal government, are not part of public and independent institutions' recruitment practices. A 1992 law prohibits colleges and universities from compensating recruiters with "any commission, bonus, or other incentive payment based directly or indirectly on success in securing." This prohibition, however, does not extend to the recruitment of international students, and some institutions are turning to outside agents to assist with overseas recruiting efforts. But, as colleges and universities in other countries become more competitive with American institutions, the viability of recruiting international students may come under pressure. The student affairs committee, in conjunction with the academic affairs committee, should discuss the institution's policies.[40] *(See page 85 for section on Academic Affairs Committee and page 95 for section on International Programs.)*

---

[40] For additional resources from AGB, see:
- Paredes, Raymund A. "How Can Higher Education Attract—and Graduate—More Hispanic Students?" *Trusteeship*, November/December 2011.
- Sevier, Robert A. "Still Dreading the Perfect Storm." *Trusteeship*, July/August 2007.

Student Health and Safety

To start the dialogue, student affairs committee members should ask:

- **Common causes.** Does the administration regularly review reports of serious injury and death, looking for common causes and investigating appropriate responses to reduce recurring incidents?
- **Alcohol abuse.** Does the student affairs committee regularly communicate the importance of alcohol and substance abuse prevention to the administration and community? Is a process in place for the administration to monitor and analyze alcohol violations and links to academic retention and student health and safety?
- **Student health services.** Does the administration clearly articulate and enforce policies on the types and levels of campus health services available to students and provide information on external sources of health care?

No higher education institution can promise a totally safe and risk-free experience to students and their parents. An important part of learning is being able to make mistakes, learn from them, and move on. But no family sends a child to college with the expectation that serious injury or death will result, and no president or dean ever wants to have to call a family about serious injury to or the death of their student.

The climate of risk-taking and personal responsibility for taking risks has swung back and forth over the decades. Board members who graduated in the 1960s and early 1970s experienced *in loco parentis* as students, where the institution acted in the role of a parent. Since the mid-1970s, this social contract eroded and students over the age of 18 have been treated as adults and institutions have not acted in a parental oversight role. Today, however, the pendulum is swinging back. Recent court decisions and family expectations are again holding colleges and universities more responsible for the safekeeping of students.

Alcohol and Drug Use. High-risk or "binge" drinking (defined as four or

Insight: The return of *in loco parentis*

High-risk student behavior may be considered to be part of moving into adulthood, but the shifting winds of *in loco parentis* and greater potential liability if serious injury or death occurs places a greater obligation on institutions of higher education to train student affairs staff, faculty, coaches, and other frontline staff on prevention and response strategies.

more drinks for women and five or more for men during one drinking session)—including all of the associated risks of hazing, assaults, falls, and fatalities—remains a persistent and pervasive problem on college and university campuses. Alcohol continues to be the drug of choice for college students.[41] According to the 2006–2008 Core Alcohol and Drug (CAD) Study, funded by the Department of Education, 66 percent of underage college students reported consuming alcohol in the past 30 days and 40 percent of all students reported high-risk drinking in the past two weeks. These numbers have remained constant for the past two decades. A study of United Educators' claims revealed that the average cost associated with a student injury or death claim was 25 percent higher if it involved alcohol.

In 2009, research conducted by Outside the Classroom and the Alcohol Prevention Coalition identified four primary reasons for lack of success in reducing alcohol abuse:

1. Low priority for senior administrators;
2. Failure to devote a steady stream of funding to alcohol abuse prevention efforts;
3. Absence of shared accountability across the institution for student health and wellness, including alcohol use; and
4. Limited understanding of the connection between this issue and its impact on institutional priorities, such as student retention, graduation, and student health and safety.

More research—including exit interviews for non-returning students and analysis of campus intervention efforts—is needed to better understand the correlation and causation of student persistence and alcohol abuse, but initial studies reveal alarming trends. Emerging evidence links student attrition to high-risk drinking; one study by David Anderson of George Mason University in 2006 identified one-third of all attrition as related to alcohol.

The CAD study also reported that 17 percent of students surveyed used marijuana, 3 percent amphetamines, and 2 percent cocaine in the past 30 days. More

---

[41] For additional resource from AGB, see Busteed, Brandon. "What Are Common Misconceptions About College-age Drinking?" *Trusteeship*, March/April 2009.

recently, student affairs professionals have noted an increased abuse of "the study drugs," certain prescription drugs used to treat attention deficit disorder (ADD) and attention deficit hyperactivity disorder (ADHD).

Student affairs committees can support reducing high-risk drinking and substance abuse by:

- Taking an active interest in alcohol and substance abuse prevention programs;
- Supporting steady funding for training and awareness programs;
- Setting measurable goals for reducing high-risk drinking and tracking key indicators of success; and
- Holding administrators accountable for student health outcomes, including high-risk drinking and illegal drug use.

In addition, recent changes in state marijuana laws bump into federal regulations for drug-free campuses, giving the student affairs committee a new topic for debate.

Student Health Centers. Based on a study of student claims, the most significant liability risk relates to claims involving student mental health issues, improper treatment or diagnosis in student clinics, and poor medical response to a student health emergency. While these types of claims made up only 7 percent of total claims reported over a five-year period, the dollars spent to defend and settle these claims was 30 percent of the total. Institutions have paid tens of millions of dollars in defense and settlement for negligence claims involving campus clinicians who allegedly failed to diagnose serious medical conditions, such as meningitis, brain tumors, and breast cancer. Likewise, similar claims have been brought against public-safety staff who were not trained appropriately to respond to serious medical emergencies that resulted in life-altering injuries and death to students.

Many of the claims concerned suicide, the second leading cause of death among college students. Lawsuits following a death or self-inflicted injury often allege that the incident was foreseeable and

Good Samaritan policies put safety first

Some colleges and universities seek to reduce the risk that under-age drinkers will be too fearful to call 911 in an alcohol or drug-related emergency with "medical amnesty" or "good Samaritan" exemption policies. Such provisions derive from state laws that shield people from liability claims when they help an injured stranger. Other institutions feel that adopting such formal policies would be perceived as condoning substance abuse and hinder campus efforts to curb it.

therefore preventable. Claims are made that college or university officials should have referred the student for counseling, informed the family of the student's condition, and offered more academic or other accommodations. Parents do not always pursue lawsuits, but when they do, the suits are protracted and painful for the family and the staff who treated the student, as well as the institution at large.

Sadly, budget constraints are moving many colleges and universities to reduce services provided by campus health counseling and counseling centers, just as demand is steadily rising. Campus care teams, discussed later in this chapter, help mitigate the risk of these claims. Early intervention and policies that involve families and outside caregivers can help share responsibility for student recovery, thereby helping to reduce risk.[42]

Student Sexual Assault. To start the dialogue, student affairs/campus life committee members should ask administrators:

- **Title IX.** Does your institution have a Title IX coordinator and does your institution meet all of the training and process requirements to comply with Title IX?

What is FERPA and when does it apply?

Perhaps one of the most misinterpreted laws, the Family Educational Rights and Privacy Act (FERPA) creates confusion with academic and student affairs administrators and frustration with many families. In an effort to protect the privacy of academic records, this federal legislation was passed to limit what could be shared with anyone other than the adult student. It contains, however, an important exception that gives institutions significant latitude in what information can be shared and with whom. The student affairs committee should ensure that the institution has established policies and procedures that enable the appropriate sharing of information to protect the health of students and safety of the campus community. The administration should ensure that faculty and staff are properly trained on FERPA obligations and understand the importance of sharing information as allowed by law.[43]

---

[42] For additional resources from AGB, see:
- Eells, Gregory T. "Rx for Students' Mental Health: What Boards Can Do." *Trusteeship*, September/October 2011.
- Abraham, Janice M. "Students and Risk: Eight Critical Areas." *Trusteeship*, November/December 2010.

[43] For additional resources from AGB, see Bernard, Pamela J. "Do Emergency Planners Know When and How to Share Confidential Student Records?" *Trusteeship*, May/June 2008.

Many trustees know Title IX as a 1972 amendment to the Civil Rights Act of 1964 and the groundbreaking legislation that opened doors for more women to participate in athletics. Since then, the legislation has expanded beyond the original scope of providing equal opportunities for women and men in all educational endeavors to address specific response and training in gender equality issues at educational institutions. Its requirements also apply to lesbian, gay, bisexual, and transgender (LGBT) students. What began as legislation to prevent discrimination based on gender has expanded to include specific requirements for training, investigations, and student adjudication on sexual harassment, sexual assault, and other forms of dating violence.

A United Educators study of student-on-student sexual assault-related claims on campuses showed that institutions are as likely to be sued by students accused of sexual assault as by those doing the accusing. This indicates that students who felt they were treated unfairly were evenly divided between accuser and accused. The study also revealed that:

- Some 92 percent of student-on-student sexual assault cases involved alcohol or drugs.
- In 63 percent of the claims, the accuser had no clear memory of the events.
- In 33 percent of the attacks, the accuser had a history of prior mental health issues.
- In 63 percent of the attacks, the accuser was a freshman.
- In 25 percent of the attacks, the accused was an athlete.

This claims study emphasizes the importance of developing and adhering to an institutional student investigation policy that is thorough, prompt and, above all else, fair. The allegations driving the student-on-student sexual harassment claims occurred where the institution did not follow its own policies and procedures, had confusing or unclear policies and procedures, did not respond promptly or reasonably to an assault report, and treated the victim or the perpetrator cruelly or unfairly. As with other aspects of student health and safety, the student affairs committee should ensure that adequate policies and procedures are in place and that they are followed.

Minors on Campus. To start the dialogue, student affairs committee members should ask administrators:

- **Inventory.** Does the administration maintain a current inventory of all programs and occasions when minors will be on campus or participating in campus programs?
- **Background checks.** Are background checks performed and training provided to all staff, faculty, volunteers, and students who have contact with minors?
- **Reporting.** Are the institution's sexual molestation policy and reporting requirements shared, at least annually, with the entire campus community?

The tragedy of the child sex abuse scandal at Penn State caused all of higher education to recognize that risks to minors are not exclusively a problem of K–12 schools and that universities must do more to protect children on campus. Senior administrators, faculty, and board members are often surprised when they learn how many minors are on campus or come into contact with the institution. Lab schools, childcare programs, summer camps, siblings' weekends, and high school student recruitment create opportunities where child molestation could occur at colleges and universities. Boundary training and background checks should be required for all faculty, staff, and students who come in contact with minors. Clear policies on state and institutional reporting requirements should be disseminated throughout the campus. For example, a hot line to report suspected abuse can provide vulnerable staff members with a safe environment to report something they saw.[44]

Insight: Know where your children are

A campus administrator at a research university reports that the institution completed an audit of the number of children involved in university activities. The report identified 27,000 children, and the administrator was not confident that the process had identified all of them.

Campus Security and Crime Reporting

To start the dialogue, student affairs/campus life committee members should ask administrators:

- **Security.** Are policies and procedures in place to ensure that security of-

---

[44] For additional resources from AGB, see Abraham, Janice M. "Heat Map: Is Your Institution at Risk? Protecting Minors on Your Campus." *Trusteeship*, March/April 2012.

ficers (whether armed or not armed) are thoroughly and regularly trained? Does campus security maintain effective relationships and agreements with local law enforcement?

- **Reporting.** Is regular training on the Clery Act reporting provided to campus security and administrators?
- **Threat assessment and support.** Does the institution have a threat assessment and care team? Is regular training provided to faculty and staff, as well as specially designated gatekeepers and responders?

While a safe, crime-free campus is every administrator's goal, managing security and law enforcement creates significant risks for every campus. At the foundation of a sound security program are thoughtful decisions that include whether or not to arm campus officers, that forge mutual aid agreements with local law enforcement, that create policies and practices that comply with the Jeanne Clery Act *(see Exhibit 16)*, and that ensure the campus security force is appropriately screened and trained.

Clery Act. The Jeanne Clery Disclosure of Campus Security Policy and Campus Crime Statistics Act, named for a Lehigh University student raped and murdered in her residence hall in 1986, requires crime reporting and notification for colleges and universities receiving federal funds. The Clery Act also requires timely crime reporting. Each school must maintain a publicly accessible crime log that is up-to-date within 48 hours, warns campus communities if there is an immediate threat, and release an annual report (by October 1) detailing crime statistics for the prior three years. Institutions are also required to have written procedures on emergency response, evacuation, and missing student notification (if they provide on-campus housing). Although a student or family cannot file a lawsuit if an institution violates the Clery Act, the U.S. Department of Education can and has imposed significant fines for violations of the act. Obviously, significant reputational damage can follow any publicity that suggests an institution ignored its crime reporting responsibilities.

Security Forces. The student affairs committee should encourage the institution to carefully review its mutual aid agreements with other police forces. A college or university should contemplate how much (if any) liability it is willing to assume for another party's negligent acts. The institution may want to have a

---

Exhibit 16: **Requirements of the Clery Act for Security on Campus**

Each school must:

1. Publish an Annual Security Report.

2. Have a public crime log.

3. Disclose crime statistics for incidents that occur on campus, in unobstructed public areas immediately adjacent to or running through the campus, and at certain non-campus facilities.

4. Issue timely warnings about Clery Act crimes which pose a serious or ongoing threat to students and employees.

5. Devise an emergency response, notification and testing policy.

6. Compile and report fire data to the federal government and publish an annual fire safety report.

7. Enact policies and procedures to handle reports of missing students.

Source: Clery Center for Security on Campus, www.securityoncampus.org.

---

mutual indemnification agreement in which each party agrees to be responsible for the losses it causes.

Each institution has to decide for itself whether it will arm security officers. There is no one right answer for all institutions. But, for those that choose to arm public safety officers, the student affairs committee should look for the following best practices:

1. **Extensive background checks.** Once given guns, they are most likely considered fully commissioned officers under state statute, with full powers of arrest that any state police officer would have.

2. **Use of force policy and training.** The college or university should establish protocols for the use of deadly force and ensure that all officers are regularly trained on it.

3. **Awareness of state law.** It is important to check with the state's law enforcement agency to see if armed guards have immunities that will limit legal responsibility for their actions.

Some campuses contract with outside security companies to provide campus security. Appropriate risk transfer language should be included in the contract to ensure that the institution does not assume liability for the contractor's actions. Enforcing the institution's standards on background checks should also be included in the contract.

Guns on Campus. Gone are the days when administrators could simply ban guns at their colleges and universities. The legal landscape is unsettled in the courts, and state legislatures are wrestling with "concealed carry on campus" laws. In 2010, in *McDonald vs. Chicago*, the U.S. Supreme Court held that the Second Amendment to the U.S. Constitution gives individuals the right to possess handguns for self-protection in their homes. Yet the court also stated that gun ownership rights are not unlimited and that it is reasonable to prohibit possession in sensitive places, such as schools. For higher education, that leaves at least two questions unanswered: 1) Is college-owned housing for faculty members and students a "home" in which each resident has the right to possess a gun for self-protection? 2) Are colleges and universities legally considered "schools" that can ban the presence of guns? Furthermore, the Second Amendment applies to state and municipal entities, not private institutions, but many state laws have gun-rights provisions that may apply to private colleges and universities.

The unsettled nature of federal and state law and increased activism of groups both for and against gun control laws presents special challenges to boards and administrators. The student affairs committee, with considerable guidance from legal counsel, should ensure that the administration carefully tracks evolving regulations, clearly communicates and enforces current policies, and coordinates the activities of campus security and local police.

Care Teams and Threat Assessment. The tragedy at Virginia Tech in 2007 brought an increased awareness of the importance of training multidisciplinary teams to respond to threats of workplace violence and spot warning signs in student academic performance and student discipline. Institutions call these teams by a variety of names: assessment and care team, behavioral evaluation team, student

IACLEA: The decision whether or not to arm campus officers relates to program

According to IACLEA:

- If the campus provides a full service law enforcement agency to members of the campus community, the officers should be armed.
- Campus law enforcement personnel who are provided any defensive weapon should be trained to the standards required for public-sector law enforcement personnel within the political subdivision.
- Campus law enforcement or security personnel provided with weapons should meet the standards established for use of those weapons as determined by the state or province in which the community is located. Clear policy statements should be implemented establishing such weapons as defensive weapons.

— The International Association of Campus Law Enforcement Administrators (See: www.iaclea.org/)

concern team, or alert team. Regardless of the name, the core functions are generally the same. These teams:

- Receive reports of troubling student behavior;
- Strive to understand a troubled student's life by gathering information from team members and other available resources;
- Evaluate the facts to determine whether a student poses a risk of harm or is in need of additional assistance; and
- Recommend an intervention that connects the student to beneficial resources, deescalates the threat posed, or both.

The student affairs committee should encourage the formation of such teams, ensure that their scope and composition are appropriate, and support adequate recordkeeping and training of team members and potential reporters of concerns.[45]

Athletics

To start the dialogue, the student affairs committees should ask:

- **Mission.** Have the student affairs committee and the board engaged in discussions on the role of athletics in the mission of the institution?
- **Costs/revenues.** Does the committee thoroughly understand the financial revenues and costs associated with intercollegiate athletic programs?
- **NCAA compliance.** Does the committee regularly receive reports on NCAA compliance for the institution?
- **Coach contracts.** Are there protocols in place to review contracts for highly compensated coaches?
- **Athlete academic success.** Does the committee receive reports on academic progress and majors of athletes?

The most common and significant risks to an institution for athletic programs come in two forms: 1) the risk that athletics overwhelms the academic mission and values of the institution, and 2) the risk of physical harm to athletes. A distant third

---

[45] For additional resources from AGB, see Pelletier, Stephen. "Campus Security Under the Microscope." *Trusteeship*, January/February 2008.

" Boards should consider and identify the appropriate board structure to help it meet its oversight responsibilities. For example, more than one standing committee may have oversight responsibilities for various aspects of the intercollegiate athletic program. These may include the finance or budget, student life committee, or compensation committee. Alternatively, some institutions might find a standing or advisory committee on athletics to be the most effective. "

— AGB Statement on Board Responsibilities for
Intercollegiate Athletics (2009)

is crowd management challenges presented to all campuses that gather enthusiastic spectators, but it is particularly relevant for universities that draw huge crowds to athletic events.

Many people point to the Penn State scandal that came to light in 2011 as the most glaring case of athletics administration and governance oversight gone horribly wrong, but countless other high-profile examples also shine light on governance gone astray when it comes to sports. Coach contracts, player recruitment, inappropriate booster club involvement, and weak student athlete graduation rates demand board-level oversight and ownership.

In 2012, an AGB report, "Trust, Accountability, and Integrity: Board Responsibilities for Intercollegiate Athletics," asked, "Why do boards need to step up their oversight of intercollegiate sports?" The answer, the report emphasized, is that "as the fiduciary body charged with being the steward of their institution or system, they really have no other option." The report offered the following recommendations to guide board engagement in athletics:

- The governing board is ultimately accountable for athletics policy and oversight and should fulfill this fiduciary responsibility.
- The board should act decisively to uphold the integrity of the athletics program and its alignment with the academic mission of the institution.
- The board must educate itself about its policy role and oversight of intercollegiate athletics. *(See Exhibit 17.)*

Medical injury is the more tangible risk related to athletics. At any given time, 10 percent to 15 percent of student claims reported to United Educators involve athletic injuries. While the largest number of claims involves club, intramural, and recreational sports, the largest monetary losses come from injuries sustained in varsity sports. While everyone has long known that risk is inherent in sports, recent medi-

Exhibit 17: **The Board's Responsibility for Intercollegiate Athletics**

Recommendation 1: **The governing board is ultimately accountable for athletics policy and oversight and should fulfill this fiduciary responsibility.**

- As the fiduciary body of the institution, the governing board bears responsibility for establishing a policy framework governing athletics.

- Board must act on this authority, establish high standards for transparency and ethics, and hold itself and the institution's chief executive accountable for the implementation of those policies.

- Athletic policy, as defined by the board, assists administrators with regulation.

- Board must inform itself about the risks and challenges of the athletic program and engage in policy questions that address those issues.

- While the board delegates management of intercollegiate athletics to the chief executive, it must recognize its ultimate responsibility.

Recommendation 2: **The board should act decisively to uphold the integrity of the athletics program and its alignment with the academic mission of the institution.**

- Policies that define the administration of athletics programs should be consistent with those for other academic and administrative units of the institution or system.

- The athletics program should be functionally integrated into the administrative structure and philosophically aligned with the mission of the institution.

- Boards should have a process in place to review contract agreements for highly compensated athletics personnel, financial information concerning athletics, and indicators of the academic progress and well-being of student athletes.

- The governing board should be informed of and consulted on issues related to conference membership, have final review of data ascertaining compliance with NCAA and conference regulations, and, on an annual basis, publicly certify that the institution is in compliance.

Recommendation 3: **The board must educate itself about its policy role and oversight of intercollegiate athletics.**

- The governing board of the institution must act intentionally to increase its collective span of knowledge concerning athletics, and each board member should be aware of the standards of behavior and regulations that apply to them individually.

- All board members should be informed about the business and challenges of intercollegiate sports, risk assessments, pertinent NCAA and conference rules, Title IX and other federal regulations, and the progress and well-being of student athletes.

- The board needs to be aware of the balance between appropriate oversight and involvement in institutional policy and intrusion into management prerogatives.

Source: Casteen, John and Richard Legon. "Trust, Accountability and Integrity: Board Responsibility for Intercollegiate Athletics" (Knight Commission on Intercollegiate Athletics), AGB, 2012.

cal and scientific developments and high-profile lawsuits warrant new high-level attention.

Concussions (traumatic brain injuries) suffered in football, soccer, lacrosse, hockey, field hockey, and other contact sports are receiving extra attention because of their long-term threats to mental and physical health. Studies estimate that up to 1.8 million of these brain injuries occur in sports and recreational activities every year. The National Collegiate Athletic Association (NCAA) requires member institutions in all divisions to create and implement concussion management plans, which help athletic staff identify and treat head injuries and allow the safe return to play of student-athletes. Most states are also adopting concussion management laws, mandating testing, waiting periods before return to play, and other concussion management protocols.[46]

Clubs. Cornell University hosts a cheese club, chess club, skateboarding club, surf club, plus about 500 other clubs and student groups. The university's vice president for student life notes, "Club programs play an important role in our educational program, as well as in programs at colleges and universities across the country. They provide opportunities to learn leadership and other life skills, as well as specialized activities that would not otherwise be available on campus."

Clubs are an important part of the student experience, and they should be nurtured. But, club programs can also present unique risks because of the large numbers of students participating in events, the wide range of activities, and the light to minimal institutional oversight of clubs. Among the high-risk clubs United Educators has been asked to underwrite are lumberjack clubs and parkour clubs. Parkour is the art of movement from point A to B in the shortest time, no matter what obstacle is in the way, by vault, jump, somersault, or other method.

Academic institutions rely on students understanding and accepting the risks of participating in these diverse activities and on the university's role in providing space, equipment, and limited oversight. The committee should encourage the

---

[46] For more information online, see:
- Center for Disease Control at www.cdc.gov.
- National Collegiate Athletic Association at NCAA.org.
- Sport Concussion Library at www.sportconcussionlibrary.com or Brain Injury Alliance of New Jersey at sportconcussion.com.

student affairs staff to vigilantly monitor club activities for potential risks, and administrators should monitor case law to determine if court decisions are shifting liability from students to institutions.

Study Abroad Programs

To start the dialogue, student affairs committee members should ask administrators:

- **Roster.** Does the administration maintain a list of all students and faculty traveling abroad?
- **Training.** Are processes in place for students and faculty to receive training on institutional policies, emergency preparedness, and other protocols prior to leaving the United States?

Although international study and research programs have been a part of the higher education experience since the earliest days, the breadth and scope of current programs and programs under development create new risks and opportunities. Two emerging trends related to study abroad programs create new risks: an increase in short-term study abroad programs and a shift from European destinations to emerging nations.

Short-term study abroad programs (eight weeks or less, often over the summer) have increased fivefold in the last 20 years. According to the Institute of International Education, in 2011, 60 percent of all college students studying abroad participated in short-term programs. These short-term programs focus on service learning projects, research, and non-credit bearing work. Short-term programs often function under the radar of the study abroad office (for example, around a special research project by a well-intentioned professor), which can make tracking, training, and accounting for students haphazard.

The student affairs committee should encourage institutions to establish procedures to ensure that, for short-term as well as traditional semester or year-long study board programs, all students, their families, and trip leaders are 1) briefed on the risks of traveling, 2) familiarized with emergency responses, and 3) advised of campus protocols for mental health, sexual harassment, and other safety issues.

Facilities Committee

The facilities committee, working with the institution's facilities staff, has five primary areas of responsibility:

1. **Helping to guide long-range physical planning**, including buildings, grounds and infrastructure;

2. **Monitoring the state of the institution's** physical plant, budgets, and expenses;

3. **Evaluating facilities' needs, prioritizing capital projects**, exploring funding scenarios, and monitoring major project milestones;

4. **Developing capital-asset preservation and renewal plans**, including monitoring deferred and preventative maintenance and modernization plans; and

5. **Ensuring compliance** with all federal, state, local, and campus rules and regulations, including safety, Americans with Disabilities Act, conflicts of interest, and the like.[47]

The risks that fall under the purview of the facilities committee include:

- Accessibility compliance;
- Auto/fleet condition/maintenance;
- Campus master plan;
- Current maintenance support;
- Deferred maintenance and life safety projects;
- Energy supply;
- Environmental health and safety;
- Space utilization;
- Total cost of capital projects; and
- Effectiveness of project management and cost control.

---

[47] For additional resources from AGB, see:
- Kaiser, Harvey H. "Protecting and Enhancing Campus Facilities: 6 Principles for Boards." *Trusteeship*, March/April 2012.
- Kaiser, Harvey H. *The Facilities Committee* (Effective Committee Series), 2012.
- White, Lawrence. "What the New and Invigorated Americans with Disabilities Act Means for Boards." *Trusteeship*, May/June 2011.

This is not a complete list; new risks will inevitably emerge, and some risks may not be relevant to all colleges, universities, and systems. The academic affairs committee is tasked with understanding the areas that pose greatest risk to the institution, helping to identify potential gaps in risk identification, and ensuring that mitigation plans are developed and followed. The committee should work closely with senior members of the administration and receive annual reports that designate the owner of the risk and document progress on mitigation plans. *(See page 131, Appendix A, for sample facilities committee risk register.)*

The following discussions focus on some of the most common, challenging, and significant risks related to facilities management and oversight, including:

- Campus master plan;
- Deferred maintenance and life safety projects; and
- Total cost of capital projects, including space utilization.

The following pages are intended to offer insights to members of the board and the academic affairs committee so that they are better prepared to explore the risks and contribute to productive conversations with administrators. The facilities committee should expect to see annual risk reports from senior administrators that designate the owner(s) of the top risks and document progress toward mitigation plans.

Campus Master Plan

To start the dialogue, facilities committee members can ask administrators:

- **Strategic alignment.** Is the campus master plan aligned with the current strategic direction and priorities of the institution?
- **Campus master plan.** Does the campus master plan address changing student needs, new technology, and evolving learning (classroom) opportunities? Was it developed with broad-based input from all campus constituents?

Boards and facilities committees are responsible for approving campus master plans. In some jurisdictions, local zoning or planning commissions may also have a role in approving a plan. There are risks not only for institutions without a campus master plan but also for those that move forward with a poorly developed plan or take short-cuts in its implementation. On the one hand, campus planning can tap into the specialized expertise of board and committee members in engineering, architecture, and real estate development, for example. On the other hand, very few businesses have a time horizon of perpetuity, and board and committee members often have limited experience in the nature and need for campus plans that encompass a 10 to 25 year horizon. To further complicate the challenges, campus needs and physical facilities may be on the verge of significant change.

Most master plans include a thorough analysis of the current state of the campus and its environment, planning priorities for the institution, an established framework for planning and decision making, and guidelines for implementation. Well-done campus master plans are grounded in two critical components: 1) deep understanding of the campus strategic plan and institutional priorities and 2) broad input from all campus constituents. The facilities committee may facilitate the process of developing the plan, but the entire board and campus community must be appropriately engaged.

Insight: Important facilities changes afoot

For decades, there have been predictions that technological innovations would dramatically change the traditional campus. Yet, decades have passed without college and university campuses looking significantly different. Will libraries continue to be space hogs and the nerve center of a campus? Will the competitive race to build bigger and better student and athletic centers abate? At the risk of making one more unfounded prediction: Important changes are afoot in energy use and learning strategies. These changes may finally reshape campus facilities in dramatic new ways.

Deferred Maintenance and Life Safety Projects

To start the dialogue, facilities committee members should ask:

- **Inventory.** Does the campus maintain a comprehensive inventory of its facilities?
- **Deferred maintenance.** Does the committee review major maintenance projects that have been deferred due to reduced funding, phasing, or programmatic purposes?
- **Classification.** Is the list of major maintenance projects classified by type of project, for example, safety/security, space renewal, and programmatic changes. Can these classifications help ensure that the right balance of maintenance projects are being addressed?

- **Safety prioritized.** Are life safety projects afforded the highest priority on recapitalization lists?
- **Energy strategy.** Does the campus have a comprehensive energy supply and demand strategy?

The decades have not been kind to college and university campuses. A building boom in the latter part of the 20th century was followed by an economic downturn of the first decade of the 21st century, creating a figurative and literal hole in facilities that may take years to dig out of. As net tuition revenue and state support declined, many campuses diverted money supporting preventative maintenance to fund other operating expenses, adding to the backlog of deferred maintenance projects. While campuses wrestled with the decrease in funding, campus buildings and infrastructure continued to deteriorate and program needs changed, creating new demands for facilities renewal.

The facilities committee plays a role in supporting a comprehensive inventory review of all campus facilities, including a breakdown of major building components, such as heating, ventilation, and air conditioning (HVAC) systems, roofs, and major electrical systems. The inventory provides a structure to assess the backlog of deferred maintenance and a road map for planning recapitalization projects. The facilities committee should use the inventory during the annual budgeting process to advocate for funding.

Special attention should be paid to maintenance projects that address life safety risks, including adding fire suppression sprinklers to residence halls, improving lighting in stairways, resurfacing parking lots on a regular schedule, and using daily campus accident reports to investigate areas that generate increased pedestrian and vehicular accidents.

Insight: Special events may be prime times for accidents

Slips and falls are the most frequent risk for physical harm on campus. According to United Educators' studies, they account for 36 percent of claims. While the costs of the slips and falls claims are only 20 percent of the total dollars spent, there is a significant increase in the severity and total cost of a slips and falls claim when the individual is elderly.

When older visitors are expected (such as for reunions, graduation, and concerts), special attention should be paid to the campus. A fall for a student may mean a torn backpack or skinned knee. A fall for an alumnus on campus for his 60th reunion could result in a serious injury that costs hundreds of thousands of dollars and strains alumni relations. United Educators has found that golf carts and inexperienced drivers, used to transport older visitors around campus, are often involved in accidents during reunion weekends.

Total Cost of Capital Projects

To start the dialogue, facilities committee members should ask:

- **Total life cycle cost.** Does the facilities committee (and full board) review the total life cycle cost of the project, including ongoing operating costs?
- **Capital renewal account.** Does the institution have a policy to fund a capital renewal account in its operating budget? Is the institution committed to eliminating deferred maintenance backlog?
- **Capital project record.** Does the campus have a history of on-time and on-budget completion of major capital projects?
- **Space utilization.** Does the institution maintain a space utilization plan? Is it reviewed when new construction, recapitalization, or leasing proposals are considered?

Too many campus capital projects are approved by boards without a complete understanding of the total cost or life cycle cost. The inability to adequately maintain campus facilities poses life safety, accreditation, enrollment, and reputational risks to an institution. E. Lander Medlin, of the Association of Physical Plan Administrators, notes that the initial cost of a new building (planning, design, and construction) is typically only 30 percent of the total cost of operating a building over its useful life. That means 70 percent of the total cost is in ongoing operations, energy, and capital renewal.

Facilities committees, in reviewing and approving major capital projects, should evaluate the total cost of the project, including energy costs (in some cases new facilities will actually lower energy needs), maintenance, and ongoing renewal costs. Additional parking, enhanced utility infrastructure, more staff, and new contracts for upkeep should all be factored into the total cost of a project.

Space Utilization. Utilization of existing space on campus takes on greater importance as the total cost of operating a new building steadily increases. Experts estimate that space utilization is, on average, approximately 50 percent for most campuses. As campuses evaluate the total cost of building new facilities or leasing additional space, the facilities committee should understand that alternatives for space utilization can offer options that support long-term financial sustainability.

Improving utilization of campus space is often a politically charged and unpopular discussion, but the financial risks of burdening a campus with new facilities (that add to operating budgets, fundraising needs, and debt loads) necessitate that attention be paid to this often-neglected area of facilities planning.

A commitment from the board to long-range facilities stewardship is a best practice for facilities risk management, and the facilities committee bears responsibility for leading this charge.

8

A CALL TO ACTIO

In 1998, AGB published a 15-page booklet, *Board Basics: Essentials of Risk Management*. In 2009, AGB and United Educators published a 28-page guide, *The State of Enterprise Risk Management at Colleges and Universities*. Now, in recognition of the complexity of risk management, this book challenges boards and senior administrators to embrace enterprise risk management (ERM) for all it can do to help an institution weather the inevitable storms as well as thrive into the next century. This book aims to help campus leaders answer not only "What keeps you up at night?" but also the more important question, recommended by John Mattie of PricewaterhouseCoopers, "What gets you up in the morning?"

Understanding both the upside and downside of risk is essential. To that end, this book concludes with 10 important lessons gleaned from experience and the wisdom of a multitude of professionals who have devoted their careers to understanding the risks and rewards of institutions of higher education.

10 Important Lessons in Risk Management

1. **Prioritize.** Spend most of the process focused on prioritizing critical risks. Risk identification is merely a springboard into these more important aspects of the process.

2. **Focus.** Senior administrators should focus their energy on high priority risks rather than on those that will have only a modest impact on the institution.

3. **Plan.** Follow through by developing mitigation plans and improving the plans.

4. **Borrow.** Use risk registers and lists developed by peer institutions (and included in this book), and interview senior leaders to verify applicability to your campus to start. Move deeper into the institution in future years.

5. **Talk.** Be ready, willing, and able—on campus, in committees, and at board meetings—to talk about the tough issues. Avoid following the timeworn code of silence on the most critical risks.

6. **Practice.** Use crises at other institutions as a drill or practice to ask, "How would we respond, if that happened here?"

7. **Board.** The board does not own the ERM process, the administration does. The board's role is to remind the administration of this and hold them accountable.

8. **President.** The president should lead the ERM effort (if not throughout the entire process, at a minimum to get it started) and stay engaged throughout the deliberations. Ongoing ERM should belong to a member of the president's cabinet.

9. **Administrators.** Each risk brought to the board must have an administration owner, someone who is accountable.

10. **Subject matter experts.** Call upon subject matter experts from time to time to ensure that the administration is not missing important trends and developments in the risk identification process.

APPENDIX A

AGB/UE ENTERPRISE RISK MANAGEMENT RISK REGISTER

The risk register lists offer broad categories of potential risk areas for senior administration to evaluate for urgency and relevance for their institutions. Some of these risks will not rise to the level reported to the board but can serve as a road map for campus administrators.

Board Governance Risk Areas

	Urgency Rating				Person to Address (If rated "1")
	1	2	3	NA	
Board member independence					
Board performance assessment					
CEO compensation and assessment					
Conflict of interest oversight					
Governance policies					
IRS Form 990					
Participation					
Additional Board Governance Risk Areas:					

Financial Risk Areas

	Urgency Rating				Person to Address (If rated "1")
	1	**2**	**3**	**NA**	
Auditor independence					
Budget					
Cash management					
Conflict of interest					
Contracting and purchasing					
Cost management					
Depletion of endowment principal					
Enrollment trends					
Financial aid					
Financial exigency plan					
Fundraising					
High-risk investments					
Insurance					
Investment oversight					
Long-term debt					
Reserve fund					
Tuition dependency					
Additional Financial Risk Areas:					

Operational Risk Areas

Facilities

	Urgency Rating				Person to Address (If rated "1")
	1	2	3	NA	
Accessibility					
Auto/fleet					
Disaster preparedness					
Maintenance and condition					
Outsourcing					
Pollution					
Safety					
Security					
Transportation					
Additional Facilities Risk Areas:					

Academic Affairs

	Urgency Rating				Person to Address (If rated "1")
	1	2	3	NA	
Academic freedom					
Academic quality					
Accreditation					
Distance learning					
Faculty conflict of interest					
Graduation rates/student learning outcomes					
Grievance procedures					
Joint programs					
Promotion and tenure					
Recruitment/competition					
Additional Academic Affairs Risk Areas:					

Human Resources

	Urgency Rating				Person to Address (If rated "1")
	1	2	3	NA	
Affirmative action					
Background checks					
Benefits					
Code of conduct					
Employee handbook					
Employee retention					
Executive succession					
Grievance procedure					
Harassment prevention					
Labor relations					
Non-discrimination					
Performance evaluation					
Sexual molestation prevention					
Termination procedures					
Workplace safety					
Additional Human Resources Risk Areas:					

Information Technology

	Urgency Rating				Person to Address (If rated "1")
	1	**2**	**3**	**NA**	
Back-up procedures					
Communications systems					
Cyber liability					
Data protection					
End-user training					
Incident response					
Network integrity					
Privacy					
Security					
Staffing and support					
System capacity					
Additional Information Technology Risk Areas:					

Research

	Urgency Rating				Person to Address (If rated "1")
	1	**2**	**3**	**NA**	
Accounting					
Animal research					
Clinical research					
Environmental and lab safety					
Hazardous materials					
Human subjects					
Lab safety					
Patenting					
Security					
Technology transfer					
Additional Research Risk Areas:					

Student Affairs

	Urgency Rating				Person to Address (If rated "1")
	1	2	3	NA	
Academic standards					
Admissions/retention					
Alcohol and drug policies					
Athletics					
Code of conduct					
Crime on campus					
Diversity					
Experiential programs					
Financial aid					
Fraternities and sororities					
Free speech					
International students					
Privacy					
Student debt					
Study abroad					
Additional Student Affairs Risk Areas:					

Compliance Risk Areas

	Urgency Rating				Person to Address (If rated "1")
	1	2	3	NA	
Animal research					
Athletics					
Clinical research					
Copyright and "fair use"					
Environmental					
Government grants					
Higher Education Act					
HR/employment					
Intellectual property rights					
Privacy					
Record retention and destruction					
Taxes					
Whistleblower policy					
Additional Compliance Risk Areas:					

APPENDIX B

SAMPLE UNIVERSITY-WIDE RISK MANAGEMENT COMMITTEE CHARTER

The following is a sample charter of an institution-wide risk management committee. This standing committee—in this illustrative example, it is called a council—is composed of senior administrators and supports the administration and the governing board. This charter is reprinted with permission from Cornell University.

Cornell University Risk Management Council Charter

Charge

As delegated by the Board of Trustees and charged by the President, the University Risk Management Council is responsible for providing oversight, guidance, and coordination of university-wide efforts aimed at identifying, assessing, and reducing risks that may jeopardize life and safety of individuals, and the assets, operations, reputation, and legal interests of the institution. In fulfilling its oversight responsibility, the Risk Council will assist the administrators who have lead or shared responsibility in managing risks within their assigned areas, in terms of monitoring risk mitigation strategies and marshaling sufficient organizational support. Further, the Risk Council will advise university senior leadership concerning strategic risks to the institution, as well as risks that fall between or above assigned risk areas. The Risk Council will also coordinate the presentation of periodic status reports to the Board of Trustees and subordinate committees which are relegated risk review responsibility.

Composition

The University Risk Management Council is a university-wide standing committee; it is vested with oversight and advisory authority, but has no executive or supervisory powers. The President designates the chair and vice chair, who in turn are authorized (by the President) to appoint the members. Individuals are appointed because of their leadership roles within the University and their informed insights concerning the control of risks both within and across their areas of risk responsibilities.

- University Counsel and Secretary of the Corporation (Chair)
- Executive Vice Provost for Administration and Finance, Weill Cornell Medical College (WCMC) (Vice-Chair)
- Vice President for Human Resources and Safety Services (Vice-Chair)
- Vice President for University Communications
- Senior Vice Provost for Research
- Associate Vice President for Campus Health
- Vice President for Finance and CFO
- University Auditor
- Vice President for Cornell NYC Tech
- Chief Administrative Officer, WCMC-Qatar
- Senior Director of Risk Management and Insurance, WCMC
- Director of Risk Management and Insurance
- Vice President for Student and Academic Services
- Vice Provost for International Relations
- Associate Chief Information Officer for Information Technologies
- Assistant Dean for Research Integrity, WCMC
- Associate Vice President for Environmental Health and Safety
- Director of Environmental Health and Safety, WCMC
- Senior Director, WCMC IT Security Officer
- Vice President for Facilities Services
- Chief of Police

Guiding Principles

In performing its oversight and advisory responsibilities the Risk Council will be guided by the following principles:

- Emphasize to Cornell leadership and governance that for "plans" writ large (strategic plans, master plans) or small (discrete projects, initiatives), proper attention must be paid to potential risks to the University's people, property, and reputation in the planning and decision-making stage

- Instill university-wide awareness among everyone engaged to act on Cornell's behalf that the recognition and reduction of risk are both a continuing concern and a collaborative responsibility
- Provide a comprehensive approach to manage risks across the entire institution
- Take stock of external and internal forces and factors that influence the university risk landscape
- Identify the main and specific risks to the university; and ensure that specific risks have responsible managers
- Enable an efficient system of guidance and support to individuals "in charge," through development of appropriate policies and assistance of risk advisory committees (ad hoc and standing), and elimination of silos which may inhibit institutional risk management efforts
- Gauge the most "serious risks" in terms of perceived impact and likelihood; and assess whether organizational and operational structures and dedicated resources are adequate to the task of managing such serious risks
- Make recommendations to the President and Provosts for areas requiring additional resources to minimize high impact risks
- Recognize that perceived risks must be balanced against risk control costs, and that some level of risk may have to be tolerated
- Review from time to time risk management strategies to assure they remain current with regulatory, operational, and legal changes as well as business and financial objectives

Meetings

The Council will meet at least once a quarter and more frequently if deemed necessary. There may be email communication to arrive at a consensus on an issue. Non-Council members may be invited to attend meetings as needed.

Reprinted with permission from Cornell University.

APPENDIX C

SAMPLE LIST OF INSURANCE POLICIES FOR SMALL AND MEDIUM-SIZE COLLEGES

1. **Property:** Replacement of campus buildings and equipment due to fire, earthquakes, vandalism, weather-related events including flood, wind and ice storms. Including extra expenses for business interruption:

   - Fine arts and valuable collections including archives
   - Workers' compensation, mandated by states providing wage replacement and medical coverage for injuries of faculty and staff performing job responsibilities

2. **Automobile/fleet:** such as auto physical damage, auto liability

3. **Educators' Legal Liability:** Coverage for the institution, board, directors and officers, employees and volunteers

   - Educational malpractice
   - Employment practices
   - Sexual harassment
   - Discrimination
   - Tenure denial
   - Violation of fiduciary duties
   - Violation of intellectual property rights

4. **Fiduciary Liability:** Employee benefit plan administration

5. **General Liability**

   - Primary: defense and indemnification from liability claims alleged by third parties, including students, visitors and guests
   - Excess/Umbrella: catastrophic coverage above the primary general liability
   - Crime: Employee fraud and dishonesty
   - Professional Liability/Medical Malpractice: Covering health care providers employed by institutions
   - Business Travel Accident: Employee benefit for faculty and staff
   - Accidental Death and Dismemberment: Employee Benefit for faculty and staff
   - International Travel: Foreign travel accident and sickness, medical evacuation and repatriation

6. **Workers' Compensation**

SAMPLE LIST OF POLICIES FOR LARGE RESEARCH UNIVERSITIES

General Liability – Primary

General Liability – Excess or Umbrella

Educators' Legal Liability –
including directors and officers,
employment practices liability and
errors and omissions

Fiduciary Liability

Special Crime Kidnap and Ransom

Business Travel Accident

Student Travel Accident Field trip

Medical Evacuation and Repatriation

Security Evacuation

Intercollegiate Athletics Travel Accident

Intercollegiate Athletic Accident Injury

Intercollegiate Athletic Catastrophic Injury

Student Club Insurance

Experiential Learning/Student Internship

Student Club Catastrophic Injury

Tenant User Liability Insurance
Policy (TULIP)

Concert Promoters Liability Policy

Student EMS Voluntary Workers
Compensation

Student EMS Professional Liability

International Liability

Professional Liability

Medical Malpractice

Veterinary Malpractice

Workers Compensation – Primary state

Workers Compensation – other states

Workers Compensation - Defense
Base Act

Workers Compensation - Long shore and
Harbor Workers

Workers Compensation – International

Owner Controlled Insurance Policy
(OCIP) – Construction wrap-up

Auto – Primary State

Auto – other states

Auto – International

Environmental - 1st and 3rd Party
Pollution

Property – Multiple layers

Inland Marine

Ocean Marine

Aircraft – Liability

Aircraft – Hull

Fine Arts

Crime

Protection and Indemnity

Water Craft -Hull

Cyber Liability – 1st and 3rd party

Aerospace and Satellite Launch

Student Personal Property

Student Personal Liability

Student Health Insurance

Employee Benefits

Resources

Bell, David A. and Judith H. Van Gorden. "Piloting the Portfolio." *Business Officer*. December 2012.

Bernstein, Peter L. *Against the Odds: The Remarkable Story of Risk*. Hoboken, NJ: John Wiley & Sons, Inc. 1996.

Choudaha, Rahul, PhD, assisted by Li Cjang and Kata Orosz. "Not All International Students Are the Same: Understanding Segments, Mapping Behavior." *World Education News & Reviews*, Vol. 25, no. 7. August 2012.

DeCrappeo, Anthony. *Managing Externally Funded Research Programs: A Guide to Effective Management Practices*. Council on Governmental Relations, 2009.

Denneen, Jeff and Tom Dretler in collaboration with Sterling Partners. *The Financially Sustainable University*. Bain & Company. July 2012.

Ewell, Peter T. *Making the Grade: How Boards Can Ensure Academic Quality*. Washington, DC: Association of Governing Boards of Universities and Colleges, 2012.

Report to the Nation on Occupational Fraud and Abuse. Austin, TX: Association of Certified Fraud Examiners, 2012.

Report of the Special Investigative Counsel Regarding the Actions of The Pennsylvania State University Related to the Child Sexual Abuse Committed by Gerald A. Sandusky. Philadelphia, PA. Freeh, Sporkin & Sullivan, LLP. July 12, 2012.

"Good Practice in Tenure Evaluation." A joint project of the American Council on Education, the American Association of University Professors and United Educators, Washington, DC. ACE 2000.

Greene, Randy, Chuck Shaw and Ron Salluzzo. "Made to Measure." *Business Officer*, Vol. 45, no. 8. March 2012. pp: 28-29.

Gunza, Nancy. "High Tech, High Stakes." *Business Officer*. Vol. 46, no. 2. September 2012: p. 31.

Hampton, John J. *Fundamentals of Enterprise Risk Management*, American Management Association, 2009.

The Health Research Institute, "The Future of Academic Medical Centers: Strategies to Avoid a Margin Meltdown." PricewaterhouseCoopers. February 2012.

Kloman, H. Felix. *The Fantods of Risk: Essays on Risk Management*. Lyme, Conn.: Seawrack Press Inc., 2008.

Kloman, H. Felix. "Enterprise Risk Management: Past, Present and Future." *Risk Management Reports*, Vol. 3, no. 5, May 2003.

Tahey, Phil, Ron Salluzzo, Fred Prager, Lou Mezzina, and Chris Cowen, *Strategic Financial Analysis for Higher Education: Identifying, Measuring & Reporting Financial Risks*, Seventh Edition. KPMG, Prager, Sealy & Co. and ATTAIN, 2010.

Mondou, Sherry B. "A Beneficial Bet." *Business Officer*, Vol. 46, no. 2. September 2012. p. 33.

National Research Council of the National Academies. *Research Universities and the Future of America: Ten Breakthrough Actions Vital to Our Nation's Prosperity and Security.* Washington, D.C., The National Academies Press, 2012.

Pearlman, Jay. "Decent Exposure: Reducing Facilities Risk in the Post-Downturn Environment." *Net Assets*, July/August 2012. pp. 25-27.

Walker, Paul L., William G. Shenkir, and Thomas L. Barton. "Improving Board Risk Oversight Through Best Practices" Institute of Internal Auditors Research Foundation, 2011.

Key resources from AGB

AGB Reports and Surveys

- *State of Enterprise Risk Management (ERM) in Colleges and Universities Today*, AGB and UE, 2009
- *AGB Survey of Higher Education Governance*, 2011 and 2012
- *Trust, Accountability, and Integrity: Board Responsibilities for Intercollegiate Athletics*, AGB with support from The Knight Commission on Intercollegiate Athletics, 2012
- *Tuition and Financial Aid: Nine Points for Boards to Consider In Keeping College Affordable*, 2011
- *Front and Center: Critical Choices for Higher Education*, 2011

AGB Effective Committee Series

- *The Audit Committee* by Richard L. Staisloff, 2011
- *The Compensation Committee* by Thomas K. Hyatt, 2012
- *The Development Committee* by Peyton R. Helm, 2012
- *The Executive Committee* by Richard D. Legon, 2012
- *The Facilities Committee* by Harvey H. Kaiser, 2012
- *The Finance Committee* by Ingrid Stafford, 2013
- *The Governance Committee* by James L. Lanier and E.B. Wilson, 2013
- *The Investment Committee* by Jay A. Yoder, 2011
- *The Student Affairs Committee* by Shannon Ellis, 2011

See www.agb.org/publications

AGB Statements (issued to help define and clarify the responsibilities of governing boards):

- *AGB Statement on External Influences on Universities and Colleges*, 2012
- *AGB Statement on Board Responsibility for the Oversight of Educational Quality*, 2011
- *AGB Statement on Board Responsibility for Institutional Governance*, 2010
- *AGB Board of Directors' Statement on Conflict of Interest*, 2009
- *AGB-CHEA Joint Advisory Statement on Accreditation & Governing Boards*, 2009
- *AGB Statement on Board Responsibilities for Intercollegiate Athletics*, 2009
- *AGB Statement on Board Accountability*, 2007

See: http://agb.org/news/statements

About the Author

Janice Menke Abraham joined United Educators Insurance, a Reciprocal Risk Retention Group, as president and CEO in 1998. During Abraham's tenure, UE has become known as the premier risk management and liability insurance expert serving educational institutions, offering in depth expertise on the unique risks and claims facing education. Prior to joining UE, Abraham served the higher education community through her work as chief financial officer/treasurer at Whitman College, and in positions at Cornell University and the National Association of College and University Business Officers (NACUBO). Abraham also served as an international banker for J. P. Morgan.

She serves as a trustee of Whitman College; a director of The Griffith Foundation, The Institutes Board, and the Property and Casualty Insurance Association; as a member of American University's School of International Service Dean's Advisory Council and the Association of Governing Boards of Universities and Colleges' Editorial Board of *Trusteeship*. She is a former president of the Western Association of College and University Business Officers (WACUBO) and a past member of the board of directors of NACUBO and the National Risk Retention Association.

Abraham earned an MBA from the Wharton School at the University of Pennsylvania and a bachelor's degree in international service from American University.

Author Acknowledgements

I would like to extend special recognition and deep appreciation to the following individuals, whom I interviewed for this book and who so generously shared their expertise and experience:

David Bahlmann
Ball State University Foundation (retired)

Edie Behr
Moody's Investors Service

Bonny Boice
The Research Foundation
The State University of New York

Allen Bova
Cornell University (retired)

Barbara Brittingham
New England Association of Schools and
Colleges Commission on Institutions of
Higher Education

John Burness
Duke University

Nim Chinniah
University of Chicago

Grace Crickette
University of California

Monica Modi Dalwadi
Baker Tilly

Anthony DeCrappeo
Council on Governmental Relations

Michael Gower
Yeshiva University

Randy Greene
Stevens Institute of Technology

Diana Hoadley
J.P. Morgan Securities LLC Advisors

Sandy Jansen
University of Tennessee

Glenn Klinksiek
University of Chicago (retired)

Nikki Krawitz
University of Missouri

Kevin Kruger
NASPA: Student Affairs Administrators in
Higher Educaiton

Larry Ladd
Grant Thornton LLP

Andrew Leitch
University of Alberta

Michael Liebowitz
New York University

Edwin MacKay
University System of New Hampshire

Michael Mandl
Emory University

Sylvia Manning
Higher Learning Commission of the North
Central Association

John A. Mattie
PricewaterhouseCoopers LLP

Jessica Matsumori
Standard and Poor's

James J. Mingle
Cornell University

E. Lander Medlin
APPA–Leadership in Educational Facilities

Mary Meshreky
Education Advisory Board

John Nelson
Moody's Investors Services

Diana Oblinger
EDUCAUSE

Rodney Petersen
EDUCAUSE

Nancy Pringle
Ithaca College

Will Reed
Davis Educational Foundation

Noah Rosenburg
Education Advisory Board

Ron Salluzzo
Attain, LLC

Chuck Shaw
Stevens Institute of Technology

Philip Stack
University of Alberta

Raina Rose Tagle
Baker Tilly

Kimberly Turner
Texas Tech

Ruth Unks
Maricopa County Community College District

Nakeschi Watkins
Yeshiva University

Lee White
George K. Baum & Company

Toby Winer
Pace University

Ralph Wolff
Western Association of Schools and Colleges

My sincere thanks to my United Educators colleagues who were helpful in so many ways. The book would not have been written without the expert advice, research, and guidance of my colleagues at United Educators, first and foremost Constance Neary and Judy Galliher. Catharine Bill was invaluable in the research and interviews. Karen Ann Broe, Jan Holt, Robb Jones, Doug Onley, Audra Meckstroth, Jules Montgomery, Mike Toohey, and Frank Vinik lent me their time and expertise. I also thank AGB and Rick Legon for taking such a keen interest in the subject, and the editorial team—Marla Bobowick, Sarah Hardesty Bray, and Susan Goewey—for their many contributions. And to my husband, Kim Abraham, who sacrificed many weekends and nights as I worked to share my experience and perspectives in this book, thank you.

ASSOCIATION OF GOVERNING BOARDS OF UNIVERSITIES AND COLLEGES

About AGB's Mission:

In today's environment, knowledgeable, committed, and engaged boards are central to the success of colleges and universities. AGB helps board members and college and university leaders address governance and leadership challenges by providing vital information, fostering effective collaboration, building board capacity, and serving as a trusted advisor. Our programs, publications, meetings, and services offer a range of ways to improve board governance and institution leadership.

Who are AGB Members?

AGB counts the boards of over 1,250 colleges, universities, and institutionally related foundations among its members. Boards join AGB to provide resources for exceptional governance to board members and senior staff. The 36,000 individual board members and institutional leaders AGB serves come from colleges and universities of all types (independent and public, four-year and two-year, general and specialized) as well as foundations affiliated with public universities.

How Can You Engage?

AGB membership extends to every individual member of the board and selected members of the institution's administration. By virtue of their institution's membership in AGB, individuals receive access to all of AGB's services, knowledge, and real-time solutions to pressing governance and leadership issues.

AGB members become more engaged in their roles; they gain access to vital information, benefit from the expertise of our skilled staff and consultants, and are better able to support their institution's application of key principles and practices of higher education governance. Explore the benefits of AGB membership and further support your institution's mission. Start by visiting *www.agb.org*.

AGB has many members-only resources online. For log-in information and password access, visit www.agb.org or contact: *dpd@agb.org*